# Dryden –
# On Counselling

## Volume 1: Seminal Papers

Windy Dryden

Whurr Publishers
London and New Jersey

Copyright © Windy Dryden 1991

First published 1991 by

Whurr Publishers Limited
19b Compton Terrace
London N1 2UN
England

**British Library Cataloguing in Publication Data**

Dryden, Windy
  Dryden on counselling: seminal papers.
  1. Counselling
  I. Title
  361.323

  1-870332-71-7

Phototypeset by Scribe Design, Gillingham, Kent
Printed in Great Britain by Athenaeum Press Ltd,
Newcastle upon Tyne

# Introduction

In my 15 years' experience as a counsellor, I have developed an interest in several different aspects of counselling and have written articles on these topics. However, these writings have been scattered in a number of different journals and books, and to date there is no one book that accurately reflects the breadth of my views on counselling. This book seeks to fill this gap.

During the last 10 years, I have been primarily interested in the following areas: counsellor decision-making, therapeutic alliance theory, eclecticism in counselling and the rational–emotive approach to counselling. In addition, my practical work as a counsellor during this period has been mainly in the 'arenas' of individual and couple counselling. This book contains the best of my writings on the above-mentioned topics.

In Chapter 1, the issue of counsellor decision-making is discussed with special reference to the issue of choosing among the different 'arenas' in which counsellors can work with their clients: namely, individual, couple, family and group counselling. This sets the scene for Chapter 2 in which the basic principles, issues and future developments in the 'arena' of individual counselling are considered, from a broad perspective.

In Chapters 3–5, my ideas on therapeutic alliance theory are outlined as these are applied to individual and couple counselling, whilst in Chapters 6–7, pertinent issues on eclectic counselling are discussed (Chapter 6) and a model of counsellor decision-making in eclectic counselling presented (Chapter 7) – both of these chapters focus on individual counselling.

Finally, Chapters 8–10 detail how my ideas on the aforementioned topics have been applied to facilitate (hopefully!) the practice of rational–emotive counselling.

The chapters in this book reflect what I consider to be the best of my writings on counselling during the period from 1980 to 1989. As I prepared them for this volume I was surprised and pleased to learn that the ideas contained within still broadly represent my current ideas on these issues.

Windy Dryden
London
July 1990

# Acknowledgements

I wish to thank the following for granting permission to reprint material in this book: Brunner/Mazel, Open University Press, Routledge and Sage Publications. I also wish to thank Jane Sugarman as the copy editor and Peva Keane for compiling the index.

# Contents

## Chapter 8

## Chapter 9

## Chapter 10

# Chapter 1
# Counselling Arenas

## Introduction

The aim of this chapter is to present the issues facing counsellors who have the task of selecting the most appropriate arena for helping their clients. A counselling *arena* refers to the interpersonal context in which counselling takes place.

When clients seek counselling, they may well find themselves being invited to work on their problems in a variety of different counselling arenas: individual, marital/couple, family or group counselling being the most common. It would be comforting for clients and counsellors alike to know that such treatment decisions could be based on commonly agreed criteria which were in turn founded upon extensive research investigation; a perusal of the research literature, however, leads to the conclusion that the current state of affairs is more haphazard. Thus novice counsellors are faced with a situation where decisions concerning how best to help their clients − in terms of selecting the most appropriate counselling arena(s) − may not be well informed. Much advice to novice counsellors seeking such guidelines is of course given in the literature, but in the main such advice is based upon the advisors' predilections and values as well as upon their way of construing the nature, acquisition and perpetuation of psychological disturbance. My purpose here is not to add to this body of advice, but to sensitize counsellors to the issues involved in the choice of relevant counselling arenas. In doing so I shall include material gained from in-depth interviews carried out with other counsellors. In keeping with the book's theme, the later emphasis of the chapter will be on individual

First published in 1984.

counselling.* First, then, how widely is individual counselling practised, and who practises it?

# Individual Counselling: Its Prevalence and Practitioners

One of the major developments in counselling in the late 1970s and early 1980s has been the emergence and growth of family counselling. This trend has been accompanied by a growing awareness on the part of counsellors of the important role that clients' relationships and environment play in the development and maintenance of their problems. To some degree, the sacred cow of individual counselling has been under attack. What effect has this trend had on the practice of individual counselling?

There has, unfortunately, been a dearth of research into how British counsellors spend their working time; a consideration of American research on this issue is thus in order. Prochaska and Norcross (1983) conducted a survey of 410 psychologists belonging to Division 29 (psychotherapy) of the American Psychological Association, and also reported on a similar survey (Norcross and Prochaska, 1982) of a representative sample of psychologists who were members of APA Division 12 (clinical psychology). Table 1.1 shows the involvement (Division 29) and the percentage of time devoted by both groups to work in the respective therapeutic arenas.

It can be seen that individual counselling is still practised widely; on comparing these data with those gathered by Garfield and Kurtz (1974) from 865 members of Division 12, it will be seen that the practice of individual counselling is not on the wane, at least not among members of the American Psychological Association.

Other pertinent, significant findings which emerged from Prochaska and Norcross's (1983) research on Division 29 members include the following:

1. Male counsellors were more involved in the arenas of marital, family and group counselling than were female counsellors.
2. Female counsellors spent a larger percentage of their counselling time doing individual counselling than male counsellors.

---

*This chapter will not deal with the finer decisions of selecting among different types of individual counselling. Readers who are interested in selecting among different brief forms of individual counselling should consult Clarkin and Frances (1982), who deal with selection criteria for crisis-intervention, psychodynamic, problem-solving and behavioural approaches. Readers who have a specific interest in psychodynamic approaches should consult Perry et al. (1983), who present selection criteria for four types of individual psychodynamically oriented psychotherapy: supportive, focal, exploratory and psychoanalysis. Also schizophrenic client populations will not be dealt with. Readers who are particularly interested in the selection of appropriate counselling arenas in working with schizophrenic clients should consult Mosher and Keith (1980).

**Table 1.1** Involvement and percentage of time devoted to work in various counselling arenas – APA members Divisions 29 and 12

| Counselling arena | Division 29 (psychotherapy) | | Division 12 (clinical psychology) |
|---|---|---|---|
| | Percentage involved | Mean percentage of counselling time | Mean percentage of counselling time |
| Individual counselling | 99.0 | 65.3 | 53.5 |
| Group counselling | 45.8 | 7.5 | 7.3 |
| Couple counselling | 73.7 | 12.9 | 11.5 |
| Family counselling | 53.6 | 8.1 | 9.0 |

From Prochaska and Norcross (1983).

3. Less experienced counsellors were more involved in family counselling than were counsellors with greater experience – a fact that is probably attributable to the recent emergence of this field.

Whilst such information is interesting, and comparative British research is needed, this type of inquiry does not reveal what factors influence counsellors in making 'counselling arena' decisions. Possible sources of influence will now be discussed.

# Sources of Influence on 'Counselling Arena' Selection

## The wider context

The wider contexts in which counsellors work often exert an influence on arena choice. This may happen in a number of ways. First, counsellors may work in different settings in which different norms of practice have developed. Thus counsellor A may work in a setting in which group counselling is commonly practised, whilst counsellor B may work in one which favours marital/couple counselling. It is likely, then, that the same client may be offered group counselling by A and marital/couple counselling by B for the same problem. There is, unfortunately, little research into the impact of institutional norms on therapeutic decision-making, yet such norms are likely to affect both how counsellors think about the determinants of their clients' problems and how such problems may best be tackled.

Second, counsellors often work in a wider context in which referring agents play an important role – for better or worse. When counsellors develop good referral networks, they succeed in communicating how they work and what clients they believe they can best help; consequently, they are likely to receive appropriate referrals. However, the danger may exist that they come to believe their preferred counselling arena to be suitable for a wider range of clients than is the case – since inappropriate cases are selected out prior to referral. When counsellors fail to develop an adequate understanding with their referral network, they may receive inappropriate cases together with instructions to treat clients in a certain way; indeed, counselling arenas may be stipulated which are contraindicated for certain clients. Therapeutic decision-making often takes place within political contexts, and where counsellors are in subordinate positions they may jeopardise career advancement by exercising their own clinical judgement.

Third, the influence of consumer demand on 'counselling arena' selection needs to be borne in mind. In America, where private practice is so common, the demands are mainly for individual counselling as shown in Table 1.1. These demands reflect consumer interest and not necessarily the merits of this way of working. The impact of consumer interest on counselling practice in the UK awaits inquiry.

Finally, counsellors may work in settings in which the nature of their clientèle, rather than client problems, may determine 'counselling arena' selection. A good example of this occurs in student counselling. I have sometimes considered that the most appropriate counselling arena for certain students would be family counselling. However, since their families often live hundreds of miles away, individual or group counselling was suggested as a second choice.

## How psychological disturbance is construed

Different therapeutic approaches imply different perspectives on the nature of psychological disturbance. A related issue concerns the influence of counsellors' views of such disturbance on the selection of appropriate counselling arenas. Counsellors tend to differ in their views on whether psychological disturbance is mainly determined by intrapsychic or by interpersonal factors. Those who consider such disturbance to be determined mainly by factors within the disturbed person – intrapsychic determinants – are more likely to offer their clients the arena of individual counselling than other arenas. On the other hand, those who view 'the appearance of a symptom as reflecting an acute and/or chronic disturbance in the balance of emotional forces in that individual's important relationship systems, most particularly the family system' (Kerr, 1981, p.234) – interpersonal determinants – are more likely to recommend the arenas of marital/couple or family counselling than that of individual.

It is a pity that many counsellors become polarised in their arguments

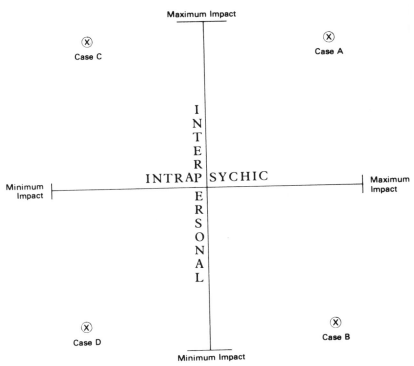

**Figure 1.1**  Determinants of psychological disturbance: intrapsychic and interpersonal continua

about the determinants of psychological disturbance when a balanced view seems warranted. Sander (1979, p.203) has written that 'the separation of intrapsychic processes and interpersonal processes is quite artificial as these processes are always mutually influencing one another'. This principle of 'reciprocal influence' should preferably be borne in mind by counsellors when carrying out assessments of their clients' problems, before making treatment recommendations. In my view, intrapsychic and interpersonal determinants of psychological disturbance can be viewed as separate continua presented orthogonally, as in Figure 1.1. Both intra-psychic and interpersonal determinants are deemed to have a large impact (high) or a small impact (low) – at the extreme points on each continuum – on clients' psychological problems. In the examples presented above (Figure 1.1), cases are described where both sets of determinants are near the extreme poles.

### Case A: intrapsychic–high/interpersonal–high

In this case, the client's psychological disturbance is determined by both intrapsychic and interpersonal factors. The client's disturbance is chronic in nature and tends to be present in different contexts, situations and relationships; in all probability the client would still be disturbed even in more favourable interpersonal environments. However, an assessment reveals that the client's important interpersonal relationships are also disturbed. This analysis suggests that counselling for this person may well involve different arenas at different points in treatment.

### Example A

Mr C. had a chronic history of depression and long-standing relationship difficulties with his wife and co-workers. He basically hated himself and was, moreover, extremely sensitive to perceived constraints on his autonomy. He was first seen in individual counselling where the focus was on helping him to adopt a more accepting attitude towards himself. A period of marital counselling followed where both Mr C. and his wife were helped to negotiate mutually agreed periods of 'together time' and 'separate time'. Mr C. was also helped to test out his inferences that he was being constrained by his wife rather than assuming that his hunches were facts. Together the couple discovered a productive way for him to communicate his frustration when he was actually constrained and developed functional solutions when this problem arose. Finally, Mr C. joined a counselling group where he was helped to assert himself constructively when he felt that he was being unfairly constrained by other group members.

### Case B: intrapsychic–high/interpersonal–low

Here the client's disturbance is determined mainly by intrapsychic factors. Such disturbance is chronic in nature and tends to be present in different contexts, situations and relationships. However, important interpersonal relationships are not disturbed. The arena of individual counselling therefore seems particularly appropriate.

### Example B1

Miss L. had suffered from long periods of morbid guilt concerning her perceived mistreatment of her deceased parents. She was happily married, and her husband was caring and supportive of her. She enjoyed good friendships and was well regarded at her job. She was seen in individual counselling where the focus of the work was on helping her to accept herself for her presumed 'sins'. She was then helped to place her 'sinful' behaviour in its proper context: as an understandable response to continued attempts on her parents' part to get her to make up, through academic achievement, for their own inadequacies in this area.

Group counselling may also be indicated if the person's problems involve specific disturbed secondary relationships (as in the following example), or if the person finds it difficult to develop and maintain such relationships.

### Example B2

Mr Y. had long experienced anxiety about his 'weaknesses' as a male. He got along very well with his parents, with whom he lived, and was happily engaged to an understanding woman. He was popular with most of his co-workers, but did not get on with two of them who habitually teased him. A period of individual counselling where his dysfunctional attitudes towards himself were explored and corrected was followed by a period of group counselling. He was encouraged to disclose his 'weaknesses' to other group members and helped not to take the negative responses of one particular group participant too seriously. The group also gave him good advice on how to respond productively to teasing when it occurred.

When significant others (those in important interpersonal relationships with the client) are involved in counselling in such cases, it will be in the role of therapeutic aide.

### Case C: intrapsychic—low/interpersonal—high

In this case, the client's disturbance is determined mainly by interpersonal factors. One such client has functioned well in a variety of contexts, situations and relationships but becomes disturbed chiefly as a result of involvement in specific disturbed important relationship(s). Here, the salient counselling arena would be one that, if possible, dealt specifically and directly with the disturbed relationship(s): for example, marital/couple or family counselling.

### Example C1

Mrs G. had led a happy life, but had recently become depressed when her husband became unemployed. Tension mounted and arguments increased as he continually failed to gain new employment. The treatment of choice was couple counselling, where they were both helped to express concern for each other in a non-defensive way and to develop new areas of mutual enjoyment. Mrs G. subsequently helped her husband to prepare himself more thoroughly for his job search, and he felt that he was once again being supported by his wife.

In another case, although the client's relationship with himself was not disturbed, his *general* interpersonal relationships were disturbed. Here group counselling was indicated.

### Example C2

Mr T. was a university student who liked his own company and enjoyed his work but could only develop superficial, fleeting relationships with other people. He joined a counselling group where he was given helpful feedback about the negative effects of his pervasively joking attitude. This helped him to re-evaluate his approach to others, and the group provided a forum for him to try out new and successful ways of relating to people.

## Case D: intrapsychic–low/interpersonal–low

The client's disturbance is due either to an acute, context-limited 'crisis' which triggers problems, or to non-psychological factors. Important interpersonal relationships are good. Brief individual counselling or psychotropic medication seems indicated.

### Example D

Miss R. was a popular young woman who had many friends and had always enjoyed good relationships with her family. She lived alone, and became depressed a month after her flat had been burgled. A period of brief individual counselling in which she was both able to fully express her feelings about 'being invaded' by faceless intruders and to accept that she was not immune from the hazards of modern-day living was successful in alleviating her feelings of depression.

This schema, which can also be applied to different problems of a given individual, is not meant to be comprehensive. It constitutes one method of making sense of complex clinical material: an attempt to integrate intrapsychic and interpersonal determinants of psychological disturbance in a way that suggests the selection of appropriate counselling arenas. A similar view has been proposed by Aveline (1979, p. 273): 'As a rule of thumb, when an individual's problem involves named people within their context then I work with that natural grouping, but if the problem is one of general social relationships, then a group is an appropriate medium, and if the individual's problems are essentially those of his relationship with himself or if a period of preparation is needed, I suggest one-to-one therapy.'

## Counsellors' preferences

Most counsellors have preferred ways of working, and this is often reflected in their choices of whom to work with in counselling. Some counsellors, for example, find the complex interpersonal transactions that often occur in the arenas of marital/couple, family and group counselling too chaotic and prefer the order that the arena of individual counselling provides them (Sander, 1979). On the other hand, other counsellors prefer active intervention in a complex field and are consequently drawn to some schools of marital/couple and family counselling. Still other counsellors prefer to avoid the intimacy and/or the emotional burden that individual counselling is likely to engender, or find such an arena unstimulating. Here, temperamental differences between counsellors are apparent and have some effect on counsellor decision-making. It is evident that counsellors should become aware of their personal preferences for working in particular arenas and make attempts to minimise the potential bias that may result to the possible detriment of client care, perhaps by referring particular clients elsewhere.

In addition, adherence to certain schools of counselling may bias counsellors, thinking for or against counselling arenas. Transactional analysts, for example, may prefer to work in groups whilst Jungian counsellors may prefer the arena of individual counselling. It is apparent, then, that counsellors will have personal preferences concerning how to work with clients and that such preferences may have a biasing effect on their treatment recommendations. It is clear that the practice of counsellors will never become 'truly objective' in that it is practised by fallible human beings who have preferences, prejudices and biases.

## The research literature

While counselling will never become 'truly objective' in the scientific sense, it would be perilous for counsellors to ignore such guidelines as the research literature might provide. Counsellors are advised to read this literature with a critical eye and to familiarize themselves with the limitations of particular studies. Consistent research findings from several sources are, however, worthy of detailed study by practising counsellors who need to consider the implications that such findings may have for their work.

With respect to the appropriate selection of counselling arenas, the research literature suggests two major patterns.

### Group counselling appears to be as effective as individual counselling

Orlinsky and Howard (1978) note that:

> In a sense this can be taken as favorable to group therapy since it produces equivalent results more economically. Yet it still seems plausible that some sorts of patients, or some sorts of problems might be treated more effectively on an individual basis while for others group therapy of some kind would be the treatment of choice. Ravid (1969), for example, found that patients who had already received a good deal of individual therapy, but who still needed further treatment, did better to have group therapy than to have still more individual therapy. (pp.310–311)

The above comment indicates the need for greater specificity in research on the appropriate selection of counselling arenas. Ideally, counsellors need to know under which conditions, for which clients and at which times a particular arena would be the modality of choice. Unfortunately, we are a long way from this ideal. Perhaps the closest the research literature comes to making a firm recommendation is in the area of marital difficulties:

*For marital problems, greatest benefit from counselling occurs when both partners are involved in treatment*

When a client seeks counselling primarily for marital problems, the research literature clearly indicates the importance of active spouse involvement in treatment. Individual counselling for marital problems when only one spouse is involved in treatment yields improvement in less than half (48%) of clients* (Gurman and Kniskern, 1978). When both spouses are involved in treatment, improvement rates increase to two-thirds. Furthermore, it does not seem to make a great difference if partners are seen (1) together (conjoint marital counselling); (2) together in a group (conjoint group marital counselling); (3) separately by the same counsellor (concurrent marital counselling); or (4) separately by different counsellors who liaise with one another about the partners' treatment (collaborative marital counselling). The most significant factor, then, contributing to a successful outcome is that both partners are involved in counselling. Although, as most counsellors who have worked with couples know, the involvement of both partners in counselling is not always possible, this should perhaps be the aim when marital problems are the focus for treatment. Of course, clients who come for help with marital problems often have other problems that are not directly related to their marriage, so some individual counselling may need to be provided in addition to marital/couple counselling. One cautionary note is in order here. In the research studies reviewed by Gurman and Kniskern (1978), it is not known to what extent the individual counselling for marital problems was actually maritally oriented. When such counselling has a distinct marital focus, improvement rates are enhanced (Bennun, 1984).

## Decision-making and therapeutic alliance issues

A consideration of the selection of appropriate counselling arenas inevitably leads to the issue of decision-making. Who is responsible for making clinical decisions – such as choosing a suitable counselling arena? Person-centred counsellors are in no doubt: it is the client. Their view is that it is unlikely that decisions about arena choice will be made before a relationship between counsellor and client has been established. The counsellor generally follows the client's lead and waits for signs to emerge

---

*To be strictly accurate, 48% improvement was obtained when American social workers in family service agencies acted as counsellors. How far these results can be extended so as to apply to different counsellors working in the UK remains to be seen.

from the client concerning the choice of an appropriate counselling arena. Thus, in these counsellors' experience, most clients are seen initially in individual counselling and when a change in counselling arena occurs the arena is selected by clients. The exception to this would be when the counsellor had strong ongoing feelings concerning the greater appropriateness of a different counselling arena; here, the suggestion for an arena change would be initiated by the counsellor although the client would, in most situations, make the final decision (Brian Thorne, personal communication).

On the other hand, there are other counsellors who hold strong opinions about the suitability of particular counselling arenas and will refuse to see the referred client in any other arena. For example family counsellors prefer to work with the 'identified client' in the family setting and might well refuse to see this person alone in individual counselling. Here, again, the position is clear: the counsellor is the primary decision-maker.

A different perspective is that decision-making in counselling is best viewed as a process in the development and maintenance of a therapeutic alliance between counsellor and client. Bordin (1975, 1976) has argued that there are three major components of such an alliance: bonds, goals and tasks. Given that a good working relationship between counsellor and client has been established (effective bonds), the counsellor helps the client set realistic goals for change (shared goals). Counsellor and client then come to a shared understanding concerning how best these goals can be met (meaningful tasks). It is acknowledged that each participant has tasks to perform in the counselling process. It is at this stage that the issue of counselling arena choice can be discussed: which arena is best suited to the achievement of the client's goals? Counsellor and client discuss the advantages and disadvantages of working in the various arenas and come to a joint decision concerning the most appropriate therapeutic arena. Some counsellors, e.g. Fay Fransella (personal communication), have noted that such discussions will obviously be influenced by the way clients construe their problems; thus if clients see their problems in terms of difficulties in their relationship with themselves the direction of the ensuing discussions with their counsellor concerning appropriate counselling arenas will obviously be different than it would if they viewed their difficulties as primarily involving their relationship with their partners. Sometimes the ways in which clients construe their problems help to perpetuate them, and consequently counsellors should be aware that clients' preferences for particular counselling arenas might serve to maintain rather than ameliorate their problems. As Sander (1979, p.208) has noted, 'patients also defensively seek out modalities that may be more comfortable than therapeutic'.

There are other obvious dilemmas that emerge from an analysis of arena selection in terms of the 'therapeutic alliance' concept. First, clients' goals change during counselling; thus when should counsellor and client make a decision about counselling arenas based on client goals? Secondly, if, for example, members of a family share the conviction that one of their members is sick ('the identified client'), how does a counsellor come to develop and maintain a therapeutic alliance with family members while refusing to work with just the 'identified client'? Here, some consider that it is often necessary initially to involve family members or a spouse under the guise of inviting them to be therapeutic aides; later in treatment, these people can be involved as clients if necessary (e.g. Dougal Mackay, personal communication). Such matters involve ethical issues – which serve as another important source of influence on the choice of arena.

## Ethical issues

Wherever the focus of clinical decision-making concerning choice of counselling arena may lie, it is important that both counsellor and client are aware of the consequences of their decision. Sider and Clements (1982, p. 1455) view the decision as a question of ethics: 'Unrecognized is the fact that with the choice of modality also goes the relative valuing of certain therapeutic outcomes.' There may well be a tendency for those who work primarily in individual counselling to emphasise the interests of the individual and play down the interests of the other people with whom their clients are involved. Hurvitz (1967) has noted that even when a client comes to individual therapy for a non-marital problem, the act of seeking help outside the marital/family unit may have unintended, deleterious effects on the client's primary relationships: a spouse may feel excluded, or the situation may reinforce the view of family members that it is really the client who is the 'sick' member. They may well then treat the client as being 'sick', thereby possibly hindering the progress of individual counselling. These phenomena may not necessarily occur, but the possibility needs to be discussed with clients seeking individual counselling before therapeutic contracts are established.

Conversely, counsellors who work with marital/couple or family units may tend to emphasise the interests of such units and downplay the interests of the individuals within them. Harper (1981) has outlined his view on the limitations of marital and family counselling. He points out that marital and family counsellors tend 'to believe that an abstraction – a marriage or a family ... is a realistic referent, a tangible and legitimate focus. Such practitioners are likely to come to think that they are working directly with these abstractions rather than with interacting individuals'. This raises the important issue concerning with whom counsellors make their contracts: is it with a 'marital/couple unit', 'the family', with each member in such units, with an individual, or with an individual with significant others as therapeutic aides (Weisz and Bucher, 1980)? In addition, when more than one client is involved in counselling, they need to realise and accept that the counsellor is not going to side with any one individual in order for productive treatment to ensue.

Let me stress again that it is important for counsellors and clients to discuss together the likely implications of each counselling arena under consideration. Sider and Clements (1982, p. 1458) have put this very well: 'we propose an honest exploration of individual and social level good in all such cases, an explicit statement of the therapist's loyalty when there is conflict between levels and a realization by both individual and social unit therapists that their choice of psychotherapeutic modality is not only a matter of personal preference or efficacy of technique. It is also a matter of ethics.'

Counsellors' ethical decisions are also influenced by institutional constraints where matters of cost-effectiveness are likely to be relevant. Pressures may be exerted on counsellors to see clients, for example, in group settings when waiting lists lengthen.

# Choice of Counselling Arenas: One Counsellor's View

I wish now to present one counsellor's view concerning the choice of appropriate arenas for treatment. I have, for a number of reasons, chosen to present the view of Albert Ellis, founder of rational–emotive counselling. He has had about 40 years' experience working as a counsellor, works regularly in the four major counselling arenas – individual, group, marital/couple and family counselling – and is one of the world's most influential counsellors.

In regard to your question about placing people in the individual, marital, family, or group therapy, I usually let them select the form of therapy they personally want to begin with. If one tries to push clients into a form of therapy they do not want or are afraid of, this frequently will not work out. So I generally start them where they want to start. If they begin in individual and they are the kind of individuals who I think would benefit from group, I recommend this either quickly after we begin or sometime later. People who benefit most from group are generally those who are shy, retiring, and afraid to take risks. And if I can induce them to go into a group, they will likely benefit more from that than the less risky situation of individual therapy. On the other hand, a few people who want to start with group but who seem to be too disorganized or too disruptive, are recommended for individual sessions until they become sufficiently organized to benefit from a group.

Most people who come for marital or family therapy actually come alone and I frequently have a few sessions with them and then strongly recommend their mates also be included. On the other hand, some people who come together are not able to benefit from joint sessions, since they mainly argue during these sessions and we get nowhere. Therefore sometimes I recommend that they have individual sessions in addition to or instead of the conjoint sessions. There are many factors, some of them unique, which would induce me to recommend that people have individual rather than joint sessions. For example, one of the partners in a marriage may seem to be having an affair on the side and will not be able to talk about this in conjoint sessions and therefore I would try to see this partner individually. Or one of the partners may very much want to continue with the marriage while the other very much wants to stop it. Again, I would then recommend they be seen individually. I usually try to see the people I see in conjoint sessions at least for one or a few individual sessions to discover if there are things they will say during the individual sessions that they would refuse to bring out during the conjoint sessions.

On the whole, however, I am usually able to go along with the basic desire of any clients who want individual, marital, family or group therapy. It is only in relatively few cases that I talk them into taking a form of therapy they are at first loathe to try. (Ellis, personal communication)

# Merits and Contraindications for Individual Counselling: Counsellors' Views

I will now consider specifically the arena of individual counselling. What are its particular merits and contraindications? To answer these questions a number of leading British counsellors were interviewed, whose views on this topic are presented below.

## Merits of individual counselling

1. Individual counselling, by its nature, provides clients with a situation of complete confidentiality. It is indicated therefore when it is important for clients to be able to disclose themselves in privacy without fear that others may use such information to their detriment. Some clients are particularly anxious concerning how others, for example in group counselling, would react to their disclosures, and such anxiety precludes their productive participation in that arena. Similarly, clients who otherwise would not disclose 'confidential' material are best suited to individual counselling. As in other situations, transfer to other arenas may be indicated later when such clients are more able and/or willing to disclose themselves to others.

2. Individual counselling, by its dyadic nature, provides an opportunity for a closer relationship to develop between counsellor and client than may exist when other clients are present. This factor may be particularly important for some clients who have not developed close relationships with significant people in their lives and for whom group counselling, for example, may initially be too threatening.

3. Individual counselling can be conducted to match best the client's pace of learning. Thus, it is particularly suited for clients who, due to their present state of mind, or speed of learning, require their counsellor's full individual attention. This is especially important for clients who are

quite confused and who would only be distracted by the complexity of interactions that can take place in other therapeutic arenas.

4. Individual counselling is particularly therapeutic when clients' major problems involve their relationship with themselves rather than their relationships with other people.

5. Individual counselling may be particularly helpful for clients who wish to differentiate themselves from others – for example, those who have decided to leave a relationship and wish to deal with individual problems that this may involve. Here, however, some conjoint sessions with their partner may also be helpful, particularly in matters of conciliation (Gurman and Kniskern, 1978).

6. Individual counselling may also be the arena of choice for clients who want to explore whether or not they should differentiate themselves from others – for example, those who are unhappy in their marriage but are not sure whether to work to improve the relationship or to leave it. The presence of the other person may unduly inhibit such individuals from exploring the full ramifications of their choice.

7. It can be helpful for counsellors to vary their interactive style with clients in order to minimise the risk of perpetuating the client's problems due to an inappropriate therapeutic style. Individual counselling offers counsellors an opportunity to vary their interactive style with clients free from the concern that such variation may adversely affect other clients present.

8. Individual counselling is particularly beneficial for clients who have profound difficulties sharing therapeutic time with other clients.

9. Individual counselling may also have therapeutic merits but for negative reasons. Thus, clients may benefit by being seen in individual counselling who may not be helped from working in other arenas. Therefore, clients who may monopolise a counselling group, be too withdrawn within it to benefit from the experience, or who are thought too vulnerable to gain value from family counselling can often be seen in individual counselling with minimal risk.

## Contraindications for individual counselling

1. Individual counselling may be contraindicated for clients who are likely to become overly dependent on the counsellor, particularly when such dependency becomes so intense as to lead to client determination. Such clients may be more appropriately helped in group counselling where such intense dependency is less likely to develop due to the fact that the counsellor has to relate to several other people.

2. Individual counselling, by its dyadic nature, can involve a close interpersonal encounter between client and counsellor and as such may be contraindicated for some clients who may find such a degree of

intimacy or the prospect of such intimacy unduly threatening and where the likelihood of overcoming this is poor.

3. Individual counselling may be contraindicated for clients who find this arena *too* comfortable. Based on the idea that personal change is often best facilitated in situations where there is an optimal level of arousal, individual counselling may not provide enough challenge for such clients. In this context, Ravid (1969) found that it may be unproductive to offer individual counselling to clients who have had much previous individual counselling but still require therapeutic help.

4. Individual counselling may not be appropriate for clients for whom other arenas are deemed to have greater therapeutic value. Clients who are shy, retiring, and afraid to take risks, for example, are more likely to benefit from group counselling (if they can be encouraged to join such a group) than from the less risky situation of individual counselling. In addition, partners who can productively use the conjoint situation of couple counselling often benefit more from this arena than from working in individual counselling. This is particularly true when they have both committed themselves to remain in and to improve their relationship.

# Individual Counselling as Part of a Comprehensive Treatment Strategy
(see also Chapter 2)

Up to now the discussion has focused on the employment of individual counselling as the sole treatment arena. Some counsellors, however, see individual counselling as one phase in a comprehensive treatment approach or as an arena to be used concurrently with other arenas.

When individual counselling is used as a separate phase in treatment, it is often employed first. From a Kleinian perspective, Cassie Cooper (personal communication) considers the progression from individual counselling to group counselling a natural one, and one which corresponds to normal child development: from the intense dyadic interaction with the individual counsellor (mother), the client learns in the next phase (group counselling) to work together with peers (siblings) and, where appropriate, to constructively challenge the authority of the counsellor (father). Perhaps not surprisingly, Cooper considers this progression to be especially helpful for clients who have difficulty in forming and sustaining relationships with peers and with authority figures. Cooper's practice is to serve as counsellor in both arenas, although the employment of different counsellors in different arenas is a further option.

Fay Fransella (personal communication) considers that an initial period of individual counselling is important for most clients. The group counselling arena, however, can be introduced to clients early in treatment, and is seen as providing a context where they can experiment with new learnings derived from individual counselling. Individual and group counselling are here used concurrently, with the gradual phasing out over time of the individual sessions used for the processing of the data gleaned from the group counselling experiments.

The concurrent use of individual and group counselling arenas with different counsellors is advocated by Ormont and Strean (1978). They argue that such concurrent treatment is helpful for a number of reasons:

1. Clients' difficulties can be examined from different perspectives.
2. Different aspects of clients' personalities are revealed in the different arenas.
3. Clients who are 'inaccessible to influence in one setting become accessible in another' (p. 35). However, such concurrent treatment is not applicable to certain clients, namely those who are pervasively anxious, severely depressed or experiencing delusions. According to Ormont and Strean, such clients tend to have an adverse effect on other group members and for this reason are better seen only in individual counselling.

Berman (1982) has written about the use of individual counselling sessions in conjoint marital counselling. Individual sessions may be indicated when: (1) therapy has not progressed for a significant period of time (3 or 4 weeks); (2) the therapist senses a 'hidden agenda' – in one or both spouses; and (3) 'a client requests private time'. Berman notes that if a client 'requests such sessions, the issue of unbalanced alliances arises. The therapist must use his/her judgment to balance the possibility of manipulation against trust in the client's sense of what is necessary' (p. 34).

# Individual Counselling: One Client's View

This chapter would not be complete without the client's perspective; thus I asked one of my individual counselling clients to reflect on the question of counselling arenas as it related to her situation. Her account is meant to be illustrative rather than representative. Amy is a 41-year-old professional woman who sought help for stress problems arising from work and, to some degree, marital pressures. My assessment led me to conclude that her problems stemmed mainly from intrapsychic factors, although interpersonal (marital) factors were implicated to some extent. Amy decided to opt for individual counselling and remained in this arena throughout treatment. Although a period of conjoint marital counselling was discussed, Amy decided against this option. In conclusion to this chapter I present her account verbatim, since it is succinct and addresses a number of issues already discussed but from the client's perspective:

As I only have had experience of individual therapy it is easier to comment on that. I can only surmise what it would have been like if my husband had come with me to counselling. Also as only part of my problems were caused by my marriage we may not have dug so deeply into other areas of me that were of more value to me as an individual. The sessions would have been, I feel, more general about our marriage and our relationship and less about my own problems.

Maybe if we had come together I should not have felt I had become dependent on seeing you. I may have become more dependent on my husband and his understanding rather than having an awareness of my own problems. Having to overcome my feelings of dependence on you has made me overcome this problem, work it out, on my own.

I know that I gained more from our individual sessions than if we had come together. It would have been interesting to have been in a group session, at some point, to discover that other people have similar problems. As I am beginning to find as I now open up to people more. It is because I felt I wanted to find out how others feel that I have been more open; if I had had this experience in a group situation I may not have needed to experiment outside, and thus not have had the pleasure of deepening several friendships.

My seeing you in individual therapy was to me of enormous benefit. I feel I needed the very close understanding we developed to be able to open up to you, to trust you. There are several areas of my life that my husband knows nothing about and these I could not have discussed because I know it would have hurt him: the feeling of being trapped needed to be examined so I could come to terms with it; my going to bed with other men, he knows nothing of, also is part of me and the reasons for being unfaithful wanted talking about; the 'need' for love to feel attractive and wanted by someone and my feelings when these relationships ended.

Part of my problems, a large part I think, was covering up my feelings of inadequacy and shithood, by grandiosity, by proving I had to and could do it all. Also by having to please people, not upset them. To really uncover these feelings and work on them needed that session where I panicked. This was caused by me suddenly realising how much I cared what you thought of me. I don't think I would have such a crush on you if my husband had been there. The one-to-one emotional atmosphere could not have developed with three people there. I know I could not have opened up in front of my husband. The admitting of how I feel about you and the acceptance of those emotions as normal, if uncomfortable, and your acceptance of me, as I am, helped me a great deal. I felt less of a shit. If I had come with my husband I would probably have been spared the uncomfortable experience of sitting in your office being very physically aware of you as a male. These sensations interfering with my thoughts. The same also happened with the tapes; I was listening to you, your voice, rather than learning from them. But I would not have had it any other way, the individual sessions I mean, as by being attracted to you, I was made aware of feelings I did not think I still possessed.

On reflection individual therapy was best for me, even if I hadn't found you attractive, I wanted that close relationship that I feel can only develop in a one-to-one situation. If we had both seen you individually for a few sessions then perhaps seen you together this would have been the better solution. As we would both have had a chance to uncover things about ourselves we did not want the other to see.

Having discussed the issue of counselling arenas in the next chapter, I consider the nature of individual counselling in greater detail there.

# References

AVELINE, M. ( 1979 ). Towards a conceptual framework of psychotherapy: a personal view. *British Journal of Medical Psychology* **52**, 271–275.

BENNUN, I. ( 1984 ). Evaluating marital therapy: a hospital and community study. *British Journal of Guidance and Counselling* **12**, 84–91.

BERMAN, E.M. ( 1982 ). The individual interview as a treatment technique in conjoint therapy. *American Journal of Family Therapy* **10**, 27–37.

BORDIN, E.S. ( 1975 ). The generalizability of the psychoanalytic concept of working alliance. Paper presented at the meeting of the Society of Psychotherapy Research, Boston.

BORDIN, E.S. ( 1976 ). The working alliance: basis for a general theory of psychotherapy. Paper presented at the meeting of the American Psychological Association, Washington DC.

CLARKIN, J.F. and FRANCES, A. ( 1982 ). Selection criteria for the brief psychotherapies. *American Journal of Psychotherapy* **36**, 166–180.

GARFIELD, S.L. and KURTZ, R. ( 1974 ). A survey of clinical psychologists: characteristics, activities and orientations. *The Clinical Psychologist* **28**, 7–10.

GURMAN, A.S. and KNISKERN, D.P. ( 1978 ). Research in marital and family therapy. In Garfield, S.L. and Bergin, A.E. ( eds. ) *Handbook of Psychotherapy and Behavior Change*, 2nd edn. New York: Wiley.

HARPER, R.A. ( 1981 ). Limitations of marriage and family therapy. *Rational Living* **16**( 2 ), 3–6.

HURVITZ, N. ( 1967 ). Marital problems following psychotherapy with one spouse. *Journal of Consulting Psychology* **31**( 1 ), 38–47.

KERR, M.E. ( 1981 ) Family systems theory and therapy. In Gurman A.S. and Kniskern, D.P. ( eds. ) *Handbook of Family Therapy*. New York: Brunner/Mazel.

MOSHER, L.R. and KEITH, S.J. ( 1980 ). Psychosocial treatment: individual, group, family, and community support approaches. *Schizophrenia Bulletin* **6**( 1 ), 10–41.

NORCROSS, J.C. and PROCHASKA, J.O. ( 1982 ). A national survey of clinical psychologists: characteristics and activities. *The Clinical Psychologist* **35**, 1–8.

ORLINSKY, D.E. and HOWARD, K.I. ( 1978 ). The relation of process to outcome in psychotherapy. In Garfield, S.L. and Bergin, A.E. ( eds. ) *Handbook of Psychotherapy and Behavior Change*, 2nd edn, pp. 310–311. New York: Wiley.

ORMONT, L.R. and STREAN, H.S. ( 1978 ). *The Practice of Conjoint Therapy: Combining individual and group treatment*. New York: Human Sciences Press.

PERRY, S., FRANCES, A., KLAR, H. and CLARKIN, J.F. ( 1983 ). Selection criteria for individual dynamic psychotherapies. *Psychiatric Quarterly* **55**, 3–16.

PROCHASKA, J.O. and NORCROSS, J.C. ( 1983 ). Contemporary psychotherapists: a national survey of characteristics, practices, orientations, and attitudes. *Psychotherapy: Theory, Research and Practice* **20**( 2 ), 161–173.

RAVID, R. ( 1969 ). Effect of group therapy on long-term individual therapy. *Dissertation Abstracts International* **30**, 2427B.

SANDER, F.M. ( 1979 ). *Individual and Family Therapy: Toward an integration*. New York: Jason Aronson.

SIDER, R.C. and CLEMENTS, C. ( 1982 ). Family or individual therapy: The ethics of modality choice. *American Journal of Psychiatry* **139**, 1455–1459.

WEISZ, G. and BUCHER, B. ( 1980 ). Involving husbands in treatment of obesity – Effects on weight loss, depression and marital satisfaction. *Behavior Therapy* **11**, 643–650.

YALOM, I.D. ( 1975 ). *The Theory and Practice of Group Psychotherapy*, 2nd edn. New York: Basic Books.

# Chapter 2
# Individual
# Counselling

## Introduction

Most counselling that takes place in the UK today probably occurs within the one-to-one arena (where the word 'arena' refers to the setting of individual, couple, family and group counselling), of individual counselling. This applies even, for example, within Relate: National Marriage Guidance, which specialises in marital and relationship problems. Thus, recent annual figures from that organisation show 149 000 interviews (of which 104 000 were with women) with individuals and 102 500 interviews with couples (NMGC, 1987).

In this chapter some fundamental principles and issues are considered with respect to individual counselling as well as speculation about possible future developments in this counselling arena.

## Principles

It should be noted that individual counsellors in the UK vary according to the theoretical orientation that they bring to the work. Whilst research on the theoretical allegiances of individual counsellors in the UK is needed, it is likely that most work within the psychodynamic tradition (Freudian, Kleinian, Jungian, object relations), the humanistic tradition (person-centred, gestalt, transactional analysis) or the cognitive–behavioural tradition (behavioural, cognitive, rational–emotive), or are eclectic and/or integrative in approach (in that they draw upon the principles and methods of some or all of the above traditions).

---

First published in 1989.

20

In this section, however, a 'common factors' approach is adopted and some of the principles are highlighted with which most individual counsellors are likely to agree (Frank, 1985).

## The relationship in individual counselling

Most counsellors would probably agree that the relationship between client and counsellor is an important therapeutic factor in individual counselling, even through different counsellors may point to different features of this relationship as having particular therapeutic value.

Individual counsellors endeavour to form a relationship with their clients that is characterised by mutual trust and respect, and in which clients feel safe enough to disclose and explore their concerns. When counsellors are experienced by clients as being understanding, genuinely concerned with their welfare, and on their side, then there is a much greater likelihood that clients will benefit from the counselling process than when these experiences are absent (Truax and Carkhuff, 1967). In addition, when counsellors are experienced by their clients as either over-involved (intrusive) or under-involved (cold, detached, and withholding) in the counselling process, these factors have been shown to be associated with client harm (Grunebaum, 1986). It should be borne in mind, therefore, that counselling can be 'for better or worse' and that what has the power to be healing has also, in less skilled hands, the power to be harmful (Strupp, Hadley and Gomes-Schwartz, 1977).

While the quality of the relationship between counsellors and clients is likely to be a central feature of individual counselling, it may not always be sufficient for a good outcome. When it is sufficient, what is likely to occur is that clients are helped by their counsellors' empathic understanding, genuine concern and respect to engage in a fruitful period of emotional release and self-exploration, where they begin to lose their fear of looking within themselves and begin as a result to explore different aspects of themselves and their life situation. It also happens that they begin to view themselves, other people and the world differently, and begin to move towards accepting themselves as fallible human beings with strengths and weaknesses. They may also begin to identify hidden resources within themselves that they may be able to use spontaneously outside the individual counselling arena to improve relationships and in the service of their personally held goals.

However, other clients may require more active help from their counsellors. Some may require, for example, that their counsellor offer a different perspective within which they can begin to view themselves, others and the world differently. Yet others may require that their counsellor help them acquire new skills with which they can experiment outside counselling sessions. When these 'additive' ingredients are a feature of effective counselling, however, they are generally rooted in the facilitative qualities of the relationship discussed above.

## A focus on the whole person

Even when clients bring a specific problem to counselling, their counsellors will offer them an opportunity to widen the focus of exploration to other areas of their life. This is due to the shared view among counsellors that clients are complex 'whole' persons. However, counsellors do not seek to impose their 'wholistic' views on their clients, and if the latter want only to work on a delineated problem their wishes would be respected.

If clients do wish to make use of such invitations to widen the focus of exploration, then the arena of individual counselling is particularly facilitative. In this arena the absence of other clients means that counsellors can offer their full time and attention to their individual clients who are thus encouraged to take an unhurried look at themselves in the total context of their lives.

A focus on the whole person not only means that clients can explore, should they wish to, any aspect of their lives, but also that counsellors should pay attention to different aspects of their client's functioning. They may, however, be constrained by their theoretical perspectives (see section on Issues). While individual counsellors are noted by the emphasis they place on clients' feelings, they may also focus on their clients' thoughts and attitudes, behaviours and skills, images, dreams and fantasies, relationships* (with other people and with the counsellor), sensations and physiological responses (if they have the requisite skills and knowledge). Such a focus also means that counsellors should neither lose sight of the interconnections among these different aspects of client functioning nor lose sight of the fact that the person is more 'than the sum of his or her parts.

This focus on clients as whole persons and on their different but interconnecting modes of functioning can be more easily undertaken in individual counselling than in other arenas where (1) the presence of other clients may emphasise the relationship between the client and others, and (2) time constraints may restrict the focus of exploration to a smaller number of modes of client functioning.

---

*In individual counselling *direct* exploration of the client's relationship style is only possible by examining the counsellor–client relationship. This arena, then, does not permit *direct* exploration of the client's interpersonal patterns as manifest with significant others (as can be done in couple and family counselling) and strangers (as can be done in group counselling)

## Explanatory frameworks and tasks

A preoccupation of some research into counselling has been to pit one approach or method against another to determine which is more effective. Apart from a number of client problems that are not often the focus of intervention by counsellors in the UK (for example agoraphobia, obsessive–compulsive disorders)*, it appears that different counselling approaches yield comparable results (Luborsky, Singer and Luborsky, 1975). One reason for this equivalence is that relationship variables are common across different counselling approaches, although it is also likely that clients find value in a diverse range of these approaches.

Frank (1985) has noted that each approach to counselling involves an explanatory framework (a conceptual scheme that provides an explanation for clients' concerns and for what is considered therapeutic) and a set of *tasks* (in which both clients – inside and outside the counselling room – and counsellors – inside the counselling room – engage in the service of clients' goals). In rational–emotive counselling, for example, the explanatory framework centres on the important role that irrational beliefs play in explaining clients' concerns and the tasks dictate that counsellors should help clients to identify, challenge and change (through thought and deed) these irrational beliefs in the counselling session and that clients should practise this same sequence both within and between counselling sessions.

It is likely that in effective individual counselling, counsellors and clients agree (albeit most often at an implicit level) (1) on an understanding of the clients' problems, and (2) to undertake to carry out their respective tasks in the service of clients' goals. The degree to which each participant accommodates to the other's view of the client's concerns is unknown but it is probable that the client is more likely to adopt and work within the counsellor's explanatory framework than vice versa. It is difficult, thus, to imagine a psychodynamic counsellor, for example, agreeing with a client that the latter's relationship concerns are explained by a lack of social skills and even less likely that such a counsellor would actually teach the client these skills (although psychodynamic counsellors may well refer clients to other counsellors for social skills training).

Extending this argument, ineffective counselling may occur when the counsellor and client fail to agree to use a similar explanatory framework. Thus, using the above example, if the client maintains his or her stance that their problem is due to a lack of social skills and the counsellor considers it to be explained by the client's conflict with authority figures, then unless one accommodates to the view of the other or the two arrive

---

*Clients with these problems are more likely to be referred to clinical psychologists.

at an explanation that somehow encompasses both viewpoints, progress is not likely to occur.

Similarly, progress may be hindered in the realm of tasks. Thus, for example, clients may not understand the tasks they are asked to perform and/or how these relate to their goals, or they may not be able or willing to carry them out. Counsellors, on the other hand, may not be skilful at carrying out their own tasks and/or may not succeed in helping their clients to engage productively in their tasks.

Some counsellors deliberately set out to educate their clients in their explanatory framework and the tasks recommended by their approach to counselling, while other counsellors do not do this. In the latter case, the client is likely to learn about this implicitly. One person who went to consult a person-centred counsellor, for example, was puzzled at first regarding what she was expected to do as a client, but came to realise that her role was 'to talk about my feelings'. She soon experienced some benefit from counselling and her puzzlement ended. In the scheme employed here, at first she did not know the nature of her tasks but came to see that she was expected ro engage in the task of 'talking about feelings'. The benefit she experienced led her to understand* one aspect of her counselling's explanatory framework: 'talking about feelings is therapeutic'. This encouraged her to continue to engage more deeply in this helpful process.

There is an important connection between 'explanatory framework', 'task', and 'relationship' variables. A good counselling relationship may help the client and counsellor to share a similar explanatory framework and an agreed set of tasks but it is not a sufficient condition for this to occur. One client remarked that he found his counsellor very understanding and concerned with his development, but claimed that he needed more active help than 'just talking'. 'I needed explicit help to change my behaviour in the real world but she didn't give me this.' On the other hand, a client may agree with the counsellor's explanatory framework and agree to perform the tasks implicit in the counselling approach but may not benefit from the process because a good working relationship has not been developed. Thus, for example, the client may not experience his or her counsellor as understanding; or may feel judged negatively by the helper.

To summarise, effective individual counselling probably involves the development of a good relationship between counsellor and client, a shared agreement to employ a useful explanatory framework concerning the client's problems and what is therapeutic and successful execution of helpful mutually agreed tasks (see Chapter 3 for an extended discussion).

## The process of individual counselling

Whilst it should again be remembered that individual counsellors bring

---

*It should be borne in mind that such understandings, as outlined in this example, are implicit.

different orientations to their work, it is likely that most practitioners would concur with the view that counselling is a process and that different interventions are needed at different points in this process. Since space does not permit a thorough examination of this viewpoint from different theoretical perspectives, I will illustrate this principle with reference to the work of Gerard Egan (1990), whose impact on the work of individuals' counsellors in the UK has been noteworthy (Inskipp and Johns, 1984).

Egan's view is that counselling is a developmental process and that different counsellor skills are needed at different stages in the process*. He further notes that the success of this developmental process depends on the extent to which the client experiences the counsellor as offering high levels of the core relationship conditions discussed earlier.

Given the above, in the early stage of the process counsellors strive to develop a good working relationship with their clients and to help them to explore their concerns in increasingly concrete and clear terms. Then clients are helped to develop new perspectives that form the basis for later constructive action. In the next stage, counsellors help their clients to set and commit themselves to goals based on the emerging new perspective of the previous stage. Finally, counsellors encourage their clients to achieve their goals by helping them to (1) develop a range of strategies for action; (2) evaluate and choose among these strategies; (3) formulate action plans; and (4) implement these new strategies in appropriate areas of their lives.

While Egan (1990) outlines specific skills that counsellors require to help them to carry out the tasks of each stage, counsellors who employ such a developmental model may use a broader range of skills than those discussed by Egan in the service of each stage's tasks. Whether counsellors are competent at using skills at each stage will depend partly on their training experiences (and partly on their personal inclinations and temperament). Indeed, it follows from this model that counsellor training programmes need to train their students in a broad range of skills if they are to help their clients across the entire developmental cycle of counselling.

## Issues

At present the British counselling literature does not include much substantive debate on vital issues pertaining to individual counselling. As such the discussion in this section will centre on two issues that I consider to be important and worthy of public debate. First, the issue concerning the pros and cons of clients moving among different arenas will be

---

*Egan's developmental model should be seen as a flexible guide for intervention rather than as a rigid approach that should necessarily be used with all clients (compare Egan, 1990).

discussed. The second issue concerns the differences among various approaches to individual counselling. The differences often centre on practical principles and rarely receive a public airing in the UK since most counsellors interact with colleagues who share their therapeutic orientation. Thus, this issue will be presented as if such a debate were to occur. This debate would help counsellors to appreciate the differences among different counsellors' approaches – an appreciation which is necessary if counsellors are to explore the possibilities and limitations of eclecticism and integration (to be discussed in the final section of the chapter).

## Movement among counselling arenas (see also Chapter 1)

Once the counsellor and client have decided to work in individual counselling, this does not mean that the client will remain within it throughout counselling. Thus, a client may be first seen in individual counselling and then join a counselling group once their intrapsychic concerns have largely been dealt with and their interpersonal concerns have come more to the fore. Indeed, some clients may be seen in individual counselling and group counselling conjointly. This can be valuable when clients need to work on a one-to-one basis and discuss at length their personal reactions to their experiences in the group.*

Should a client's individual counsellor also be his or her counsellor in another arena? Since initially clients in group counselling are generally strangers to each other, this issue can largely be explored and decided on the basis of the client's feelings and opinions alone. However, when movement from individual counselling is being considered, it is often inadvisable for the client's individual counsellor to act as counsellor to the convened couple or family. One reason for this is due to the fact that the counsellor–client dyad has a history, the content of which is unknown to the other partner or family members. The latter may feel, as a result, that the counsellor may have a stronger alliance with the client than with them and the development of a productive counselling relationship among participants in the couple or family counselling arena may thus be inhibited.† The longer the client has worked in individual counselling, the more likely it is that this will be an issue for the other client(s). Also, given that the client's partner or other family members are part of the client's everyday world, the client may find sharing the counsellor in the new

---

*It should be noted, however, that some counsellors argue that the conjoint use of individual and group counselling inhibits clients from dealing with their experiences of the group in the group.

†This phenomenon can also occur in group counselling, but is much less likely to be an inhibiting factor on the ensuing group process.

arena much more difficult than he or she would with strangers in group counselling.

In addition, issues of confidentiality may add to this tension. If a counsellor has been working with a woman in individual counselling, he or she is bound to keep confidential material that has arisen in that arena. If the counsellor then were to see the woman and her husband in couple counselling, then the husband will know that the counsellor cannot disclose this material and may feel the three-person alliance to be unbalanced against him. Such issues need to be kept firmly in mind when discussing movement among counselling arenas with clients.

## Different emphases among differing approaches to individual counselling

In the first section of this chapter, some general principles were outlined about individual counselling that arise from taking a 'common factors' approach (Frank, 1985). However, it is important not to deny that there are differences among the various approaches to individual counselling that are currently practised in the UK. These differences may make it difficult for counsellors with diverse orientations to communicate effectively with one another unless these differences are understood and, if possible, accepted. Applicants to training courses, in particular, need to be made aware of understanding these differences if they are to make informed decisions concerning their choices for initial counsellor training. In addition, if the field is to move towards an integrative or eclectic position, an appreciation of the different emphases in the major counselling traditions will facilitate the exploration of the possibilities and limits of integration and eclecticism in individual counselling. This will be considered more fully in the final section.

### Modality focus

Although it was argued earlier that many counsellors adopt a whole-person focus in their work, various counselling approaches place differential emphasis on the seven modalities of human functioning outlined in the section on 'Principles' (i.e. behaviour, affect, sensation, imagery, cognition, interpersonal relationships and physiological functioning). Thus, humanistic approaches to counselling focus particularly on affect, phenomenally based cognitions about self and interpersonal relationships; psychodynamic approaches do not place a direct focus on any of the modalities but look for the existence of unconscious conflict as it is manifested in the modalities; whilst cognitive–behavioural approaches tend to emphasise cognition, imagery and behaviour while considering affect to be the product of cognitive processes.

*Image of relationship*

The major traditions within counselling tend to consider the relationship between counsellor and client in different ways. Psychodynamic approaches view the counsellor–client relationship as an 'as if' one where the emphasis is on perceptual, affective and interactional distortions; where, for example, the client unconsciously views and relates to the counsellor 'as if' the latter were a significant person, usually from the client's past. The 'real' relationship between counsellor and client is considered to be important but as a backdrop enabling the counsellor and client to stand back and reflect on the meaning of the client's distortions.

In the humanistic approaches (and particularly so in person-centred counselling) the emphasis is on the real, present relationship between counsellor and client which is seen as the major vehicle for therapeutic change. The important curative factor in the person-centred approach is the client's experience of the counsellor as a person in his or her own right who is understanding and genuinely concerned for the development of the client. The focus on the 'as if' quality of the relationship is consequently played down.

In cognitive–behavioural approaches, the relationship between counsellor and client is regarded as a real present-centred relationship which serves as a facilitative backdrop to the successful execution of a set of important therapeutic tasks. Such counsellors are likely to view themselves primarily as educators whose major role is to help clients acquire cognitive and behavioural skills that they then practise between counselling sessions.

*Time and space focus*

Counsellors from the major traditions also differ concerning the focus they place on issues of time and space in engaging their clients in exploration in counselling. With respect to *time* counsellors may facilitate clients' exploration of their past, present and/or future. With respect to *space*, some counsellors may place a greater emphasis on interaction within the counselling relationship, whilst others may focus more on clients' lives outside of the counselling sessions.

Psychodynamic counsellors tend to view clients' functioning in terms of the latters' past experiences and encourage them to understand that their present and future aspirations are coloured by their past. In addition, they tend to seek clues to their clients' current relationship difficulties in terms of the clients' relationship with their counsellors (the transference relationship). When the transference relationship is manifest, this is then linked to clients' past and present relationships outside the counselling arena. This dual focus is well expressed in the title of Jacobs's (1986) book on psychodynamic counselling, *The Presenting Past*.

Person-centred counsellors (who probably represent the majority of

30/

humanistic counsellors) tend to work in time and space frame by their clients. Thus, they weave between the present, pa time frames and between the 'in here' and 'out there' space f counsellors, on the other hand, tend to emphasise the 'here ; and time frames in their work and endeavour to help the focus on u. frames as far as possible.

Cognitive–behavioural counsellors tend to work within the present and future time frames and focus more on their clients' outside experiences than on their experiences within the counselling room, although the latter focus is not neglected when it becomes salient.

At present, counsellor training programmes tend to be based on one of the major traditions as listed above. Whether this will continue in the future depends on the extent to which counsellors can explore how far eclectic and integrative counselling is possible. This exploration, as has been noted, will include discussion about the issues raised in this portion of the present chapter.

# Future Developments

### Eclecticism and integration (see also Chapters 6 and 7)

It is likely that in future individual counsellors will become increasingly interested in exploring the prospects and possibilities of eclecticism and integration. Eclecticism defines the practice of counsellors who claim to choose what appears to be best from diverse counselling systems, sources and styles. Eclectics often state a dislike for working within a single orientation, select from two or more theories, and believe that no present theory is adequate to explain or predict all of the phenomena that counsellors observe (Norcross, 1986).

Integration, on the other hand, refers to the process of incorporating parts into a whole and stresses the formulation of a perspective on counselling that emphasises common factors within a generally accepted overarching framework. Integrationists, like eclectics, are disenchanted with a single theoretical approach to counselling but are more preoccupied than eclectics with integrating the endeavours of counsellors from disparate schools.

There are signs that the trend away from single counselling systems is beginning to get underway in the UK; for example, there exists a growing UK network of members of the Society for the Exploration of Psychotherapy Integration (SEPI). However, a caution is in order at this point. To call yourself an eclectic or an integrationist reveals nothing about your mode of practice. These terms may be fashionable but it is important that they do not obscure undisciplined practice. Indeed, eclectics, for example, are often perceived as muddle-headed individuals who are too sloppy or lazy

⌐ develop a sound set of theoretical principles to guide their work. It may be that for the development of a mature eclecticism or integrationism in individual counselling to occur practitioners need to have either sound initial training in one theoretical approach to counselling while being exposed to the merits of other approaches or a sound training in one eclectic or integrative approach of counselling – for example, that based on Egan's (1990) work. However, such developments will also be enhanced by a much-needed growth in more advanced training courses in counselling (in both the public and private educational sectors) where experienced practitioners might come together to explore the possibilities of eclecticism and integration.   What are the issues that such individuals might explore in such forums? These could include the development of:

1.  A set of common principles, couched in acceptable language, that could form the basis of further exploration.
2.  A matrix of modalities of client functioning that would facilitate comprehensiveness in individual counselling. Lazarus (1981) has outlined one such matrix that was referred to earlier in this chapter, for example, behaviour, affect, sensation, imagery, cognition, interpersonal relationships and physiological functioning.
3.  Salient dimensions of client variability to enable counsellors to consider how they might vary their practice in response to such client variability. Beutler (1983), for example, has argued that symptom complexity, level of client reactance (to therapeutic influence) and style of defence constitute important dimensions along which clients vary and which merit a differential counsellor response. To this list might be added an understanding of clients' learning styles and how they may warrant modifications in counselling approach.
4.  A schema for counsellor decision-making allied to a taxonomy of salient dimensions of client variability that would help practitioners make decisions concerning, for example, variations in interactional style, modifications in the therapeutic alliance, and selection among a set of counselling methods and techniques.

It is apparent that putting these points together in a consistent and productive manner constitutes an immense task, but I predict that exploration in this area will be along these lines out of which counsellors will discover the advantages and disadvantages of eclectic and integrative practice.

Individual counselling is a particularly appropriate arena in which the development of these ideas can be explored. Thus, for example, if counsellors are going to consider how to vary their approach to clients across the counselling process then this is best done, at least initially, in the arena of individual counselling where practitioners do not have to consider the impact that such variation might have on other clients present.

## Specialised versus generalised counselling

Most individual counsellors working currently in the UK are likely to be generalists but with one or more particular specialisms. They are trained (within the constraints of particular counselling orientations) to offer general counselling to clients with a range of concerns and difficulties, but in the course of their work may come to specialise in working with a particular group of clients. As shown elsewhere in this volume, working with particular client groups involves a detailed knowledge of the specific concerns and issues that face these groups. However, to what extent does working with particular client groups involve modification of one's general counselling approach? There is a need to translate careful delineation of particular clients' problems and issues into the development of specific counselling interventions targeted for use with these clients and I predict that this is one area in which individual counselling will develop in the future. If the development can be harnessed to those in the area of eclecticism/integration, then the likelihood that a personalised counselling approach will be offered to clients who have specialised needs (with regard to their concerns) and individual needs (with respect to their learning styles, and so on) will be increased.

## Addressing the 'plastic bubble' effect

Critics of individual counselling have argued that there is a danger that a kind of 'plastic bubble' surrounds work that is done in this counselling arena, in that the work may become isolated from the realities of the client's life. Whilst I have shown that movement among different counselling arenas can (and, some would argue, should) occur to obviate this effect, what can the counsellor do to weaken the boundary between individual counselling and the client's everyday life? I foresee that individual counsellors will increasingly grapple with this problem, especially as issues of accountability and effectiveness with respect to counselling in general and individual counselling in particular come more to the fore in British society. It is likely, then, that individual counsellors will experiment with modifications in their approach, such as (1) incorporating interventions that *specifically* address the generalisation issue (i.e. how clients can specifically use their counselling-inspired gains in their daily lives), and (2) utilising interventions that treat absent significant others 'as if' they were present. Bennun's (1985) description of doing marital counselling when only one partner is present is a good example of this latter trend.

# Conclusion

To what extent these and other developments in individual counselling will occur depends on the willingness of counsellors to:

1. Adopt an experimental attitude to their work.
2. Read widely the literature on counselling (including that from North America where, in the author's view, most creative developments still seem to originate).
3. Learn from each other's innovations.

Given the great strides that counselling in the UK has made in the 1980s, the future prospects for individual counselling look most promising.

# References

BENNUN, I. (1985). Unilateral marital therapy. In Dryden, W. (Ed.) *Marital Therapy in Britain*, Volume 2: *Special Areas*. London: Harper & Row.

BEUTLER, L.E. (1983). *Eclectic Psychotherapy: A systematic approach*. New York: Pergamon.

DRYDEN, W. (1984). Therapeutic arenas. In Dryden, W. (Ed.) *Individual Therapy in Britain*. London: Harper & Row.

EGAN, G. (1990). *The Skilled Helper: A systematic approach to effective helping*, 4th edn. Monterey, CA: Brooks/Cole.

FRANK, J.D. (1985). Therapeutic components shared by all psychotherapies. In Mahoney, M.J. and Freeman, A. (Eds) *Cognition and Psychotherapy*. New York: Plenum.

GRUNEBAUM, H. (1986). Harmful psychotherapy experience. *American Journal of Psychotherapy* 40, 165–176.

GURMAN, A.S. and KNISKERN, D.P. (1978). Research in marital and family therapy. In Garfield, S.L. and Bergin, A.E. (Eds) *Handbook of Psychotherapy and Behavior Change*, 2nd edn. New York: Wiley.

INSKIPP, F. and JOHNS, H. (1984). Developmental eclecticism: Egan's skills model of helping. In Dryden, W. (Ed.) *Individual Therapy in Britain*. London: Harper & Row.

JACOBS, M. (1986). *The Presenting Past*. London: Harper & Row.

LAZARUS, A.A. (1981). *The Practice of Multimodal Therapy*. New York: McGraw-Hill.

LUBORSKY, L., SINGER, B. and LUBORSKY, L. (1975). Comparative studies of psychotherapy: is it true that 'everyone has won and all must have prizes'? *Archives of General Psychiatry* 32, 995–1008.

NMGC (1987). *The Annual Review of the National Marriage Guidance Council*. Rugby: NMGC.

NORCROSS, J.C. (1986). Eclectic psychotherapy: an introduction and overview. In Norcross, J.C. (Ed.) *Handbook of Eclectic Psychotherapy*. New York: Brunner/Mazel.

RAVID, R. (1969). Effect of group therapy on long-term individual therapy. *Dissertation Abstracts International* 30, 2427B.

STRUPP, H.H., HADLEY, S.W. and GOMES-SCHWARTZ, B. (1977). *Psychotherapy for Better or Worse: The problem of negative effects*. New York: Aronson.

TRUAX, C.B. and CARKHUFF, R.R. (1967). *Toward Effective Counseling and Psychotherapy: Training and practice*. Chicago: Aldine.

# Chapter 3
# The Therapeutic Alliance as an Integrating Framework in Individual Counselling

In this chapter I will consider a perspective on the therapeutic alliance in individual counselling which, I believe, can serve as an integrating framework to help counsellors intervene sensitively throughout the counselling process. The view which asserts that counselling is a process which unfolds over time is, in my view, a crucial one. Counsellors are faced with different challenges at the beginning of counselling than they are during the middle and ending stages of this helping endeavour. Effective counsellors, then, are those who are flexible and skilful enough to modify their interventions according to the particular stage in which they and their clients are working. Effective counsellors also can vary their style of intervention according to the different needs of different clients.

## The Therapeutic Alliance as an Integrating Framework

Bordin (1979) has written an important paper showing how the old psychoanalytical concept of the working alliance between counsellor and client (here referred to as the therapeutic alliance) can be broadened and divided into interrelated components. He argued that the therapeutic alliance – the interpersonal connectedness between counsellor and client – can be broken down into three such components: bonds, goals and tasks.

## Bonds

When the *bond* between counsellor and client becomes a focus for consideration, certain counselling concepts are brought into view. The first, and perhaps the one that has received most attention in the literature,

First published in 1989.

concerns the interpersonal attitudes of the counsellor and their impact on
the client. Such work has its roots in the person-centred tradition (Mearns
and Thorne, 1988) but has a wider relevance. This work has shown that
when the counsellor (1) demonstrates an empathic understanding of the
client's concerns, (2) is genuine in the therapeutic encounter and (3)
shows unconditional acceptance of the client as a person, and when the
client experiences the presence of these counsellor-offered conditions,
then the client tends to move to a position of greater psychological growth.
Early arguments that such communicated (and perceived) counsellor
attitudes were necessary and sufficient for client development have
subsequently given way to the view that these attitudes are therapeutic
under most but not all conditions. Indeed it is interesting to compare the
views of Mearns and Thorne (1988) with those of Trower, Casey and
Dryden (1988) on this point. For Mearns and Thorne such counsellor
attitudes form the backbone of their book on person-centred counselling
and the skilful communication of these attitudes constitutes the basic work
of person-centred counsellors. For Trower, Casey and Dryden who write
on cognitive–behavioural counselling, these attitudes are important in that
they set the stage for the strategic and technical work that is to follow.

From a therapeutic alliance perspective, a more complex picture
emerges that is in keeping with the present research position (see Beutler,
Crago and Arizmendi, 1986). This position states that these counsellor
attitudes are often important for most but not all clients. Here the task of
the counsellor is to emphasise certain attitudes with some clients and to
de-emphasise other attitudes with other clients in order to establish the
most productive and idiosyncratic therapeutic bond with each individual
client.

The second area that is relevant to the discussion of the therapeutic
bond places more attention on the client's feelings and attitudes towards
the counsellor. Here such concepts as the client's trust in the counsellor,
feelings of safety in the relationship, and degree of faith in the counsellor
as a persuasive change agent become salient. Whilst the focus of
understanding how best to promote such client feelings and attitudes has
been on constructive counsellor qualities and interventions, it is becoming
increasingly recognised that clients bring with them to the counselling
endeavour pre-formed tendencies in these areas which have a powerful
impact on the counselling process (Moras and Strupp, 1982). Thus it may
be that when a client has little trust in other people, finds them threatening
to be with and has little or no faith in counselling as a vehicle for personal
change, then the phenomenon of 'client reluctance' is encountered. This
is particularly so when, in addition, the client has, in some way, been
coerced into seeking counselling 'help'.

The third area relevant to the therapeutic bond concerns work that has
been done on the interpersonal styles of both client and counsellor. Here

the focus is more interactive than in the previous two areas. The line of reasoning that has emerged from such work is that the counselling bond can be enhanced when the 'fit' between the interpersonal styles of counsellor and client is good and threatened when such a fit is poor. An example of a productive fit between counsellor and client, at least in the early stages of the relationship would be when the counsellor's style is 'dominant–friendly' and the client's style is 'submissive–friendly'. An example of an unproductive fit would be when the counsellor's style is 'passive–neutral' and the client's, 'submissive–hostile'. The implications from such work are that the counsellor's initial task is to modify his or her interpersonal style to complement the client's style in order to initiate the therapeutic alliance. Once such an alliance has been firmly established, the counsellor can begin to consider ways of slowly changing his or her style in the service of initiating client change. The important point here is that initial bonds which may be counter-therapeutic in the longer term for client development may have to be established to get the relationship off the ground.

Another implication of this work is that clients who have a critical/hostile style of interaction are more difficult to engage in counselling at the outset than clients who are appreciative/friendly. Whilst the danger here is that clients who are critical and hostile get blamed for prematurely dropping out of counselling, the real implications of such a viewpoint concern alerting counsellors to very early signs of threat to the development of a productive alliance and encouraging them to focus on this in as constructive a way as possible. Indeed it has been shown that ignoring such threats does little to promote a constructive counselling relationship (Foreman and Marmar, 1985).

Another slightly different way of looking at the counsellor–client interactive bond has emerged from social psychology (Dorn, 1984). Here the focus has been on clients' expectations for counsellor participation and counsellors' use of a power base particularly in the early stage of counselling.

When clients show a preference for counsellor formality and demonstrations of expertise, then counsellors who seek to meet such expectations, at least initially, are more successful at initiating a productive therapeutic alliance than counsellors who try to encourage the clients to work in a relationship characterised by counsellor informality and friendliness. Clients who have such expectations seem to benefit more at the outset when counsellors use a power base consonant with these expectations. In this case, this means emphasising one's credibility as an expert and using a formal style of interaction. However, using such a power base may well have an impeding effect on clients who expect their counsellor to be more informal in style and to emphasise personal rather than professional qualities. With such clients, counsellors need to emphasise a power base characterised by informality, attractiveness and trustworthiness.

The point here is that counsellors who can appropriately vary their style of interaction and the power base in which such styles are rooted, are more likely to be more successful at initiating a therapeutic alliance than counsellors who use only one style of interaction and a single power base and expect their clients to adjust accordingly.

The final area which is relevant to the bond between counsellor and client relates to the concepts of transference and counter-transference. Although these concepts have been derived from psychoanalytical approaches to counselling and psychotherapy (see Jacobs, 1988) and their very mention has a negative effect on many non-analytically oriented counsellors, my position is that it is the phenomena to which the terms point that are more crucial than the use of terms themselves. The terms point to the fact that both clients and counsellors bring to the counselling relationship tendencies to perceive, feel and act towards another person which are influenced by their prior interaction with significant others. These tendencies can and often do have a profound influence on the development and maintenance of the therapeutic alliance.

Watkins (in Dryden, 1989) has aptly summarised the major ways in which such tendencies become manifest in the counselling relationship, and whichever terms one uses to describe such phenomena, the phenomena require understanding and constructive handling on the part of the counsellor.

It should not be forgotten that the development, maintenance and ending of the therapeutic bond (as with the other components of the therapeutic alliance to be considered) are influenced by the gender and racial composition of the counsellor–client pairing and I refer the reader to Chaplin (1988) and d'Ardenne and Mahtani (1989) for a full discussion of these issues.

Bordin's (1979) point about the importance of bonds in the therapeutic alliance is that the effectiveness of counselling and psychotherapy depends, to a large extent, on the development and maintenance of a productive bond between counsellor and client. I would like to stress here, as I have done earlier, that while the distinguishing feature of the bond in its early stages is one where there is a comfortable fit between counsellor and client, productive change is more often predicated upon the resolution of manageable conflict in the bond than it is on the perpetuation of early feelings of comfort in that relationship, although it has to be said that some clients do benefit considerably from counselling relationships which are characterised by an enduring sense of comfort. Yet in most counselling relationships the counsellor needs to introduce dissonant elements (challenges) into the relationship so that the client can be encouraged to make changes in his or her style of acting, feeling and thinking.

Such dissonant elements or challenges, when constructive, need to be introduced in the context of a relationship based on solid foundations, i.e. solid enough to survive the challenges thus introduced. The challenge may indeed be introduced by the client and Bordin makes the important point that from wherever the challenge originates the therapeutic alliance may indeed be strengthened by the successful resolution of a threat to its existence. It is where such a solid foundation in the relationship is absent that challenges have the greatest potential for therapeutic harm for the client (and, in some instances, the counsellor).

# Goals

The second component of the therapeutic alliance – goals – pertains to the objectives both client and counsellor have for coming together in the alliance. Goals are therefore the raison d'être of the counselling process. At first the issue of goals in the therapeutic alliance may seem deceptively simple: the client is in some kind of psychological distress, wants relief from this distress and wishes to live a more fulfilling life. The counsellor's goal is to help the client achieve his or her goals. However, the situation is often more complex than this and there are a number of issues that need to be discussed when goals become centre stage for consideration in the therapeutic alliance.

Before considering these issues, let us consider Bordin's (1979) major point about goals and use this as a starting point for considering the complexity of the subject. Bordin has argued that a good therapeutic outcome is facilitated when the counsellor and client agree what the client's goals are, and agree to work towards the fulfilment of these goals. Thus Bordin is concerned basically with outcome goals, i.e. goals which are set as a criterion for the success, potential success or failure of the counselling encounter at its end.

Whether such agreement over clients' goals should be explicit or implicit is a theme taken up by Sutton (in Dryden, 1989) who is quite clear that goals should be explicitly set after the therapeutic bond has been initiated and after a period of initial assessment has been concluded.

Bordin's point alerts us to potential sources of failure and/or obstacles to the development of the counselling process. Thus the therapeutic alliance is threatened when either explicitly, or perhaps more commonly implicitly, the counsellor and client have different outcome goals in mind for the client.

This may occur for a variety of reasons. It often stems from prior disagreement, again often covert, concerning either how counsellor and client define the latter's problem or how the two account for the existence of the problem and how it is being maintained. An example of disagreement concerning problem definition is when the client considers that he or she has an anxiety problem whereas the counsellor considers that the client's problem is basically one of depression. As a result the alliance is threatened because when the client wishes to focus on his or her anxiety the counsellor wishes to focus on his or her presumed depression.

How can the counsellor and client deal with such a threat to the alliance? Obviously the first way is for the counsellor to realise that the threat exists and to assess correctly the source of that threat. But even then, and this is a point which I wish to underscore, there has to be some mechanism for the threat to be discussed. Of course the counsellor can make an adjustment in his or her view of the client's goals on the basis of a correct assessment without this being discussed. But here I wish to focus on the ensuing discussion between client and counsellor.

A productive feature of counselling exists, in my opinion, when client and counsellor can step back from the work that is being done and reflect together on the nature and effects of this work. If one thinks of both counsellor and client as having an experiencing part of themselves and an observing part (which can stand back and reflect on what has been experienced) then this process of reflection (called henceforth the reflection process) involves both client and counsellor stepping back and using the observing parts of themselves to reflect on what has gone before.

Coming back to the example, the counsellor and client can reflect (during the reflection process) on the counselling process and can begin to search for the source(s) of this threat to the alliance. If they both recognise that they differ concerning the nature of the client's basic problem, they can begin to talk about this and renegotiate a common as opposed to a disparate view of the problem. Without such a reflection process being part of the counselling relationship, the possibilities for reducing conflict occasioned by such differing viewpoints are reduced. Indeed, the establishment and maintenance of this reflection process means that counsellor and client have a forum for dealing with potential threats to the alliance in all three of its domains: bonds, goals and tasks.

Returning to the theme, if the counsellor and client agree (or come to agree) on a common definition of the client's problem they may still have differing views concerning how to account for this problem and its maintenance. It is here that counsellors are particularly influenced by their dominant theoretical orientation to counselling. Thus a cognitive–behavioural counsellor may have a very different view of the client's problem (see Trower, Casey and Dryden, 1988) from, for example, a psychodynamically orientated counsellor (see Jacobs, 1988). The important issue, from an alliance perspective, is not the inherent validity of one view over another; rather it is whether or not the counsellor and client share a common conceptualisation of the client's problem which will enable the work to proceed.

Referring the issue for discussion to the reflection process is again advocated here. The outcome of such discussion may be for the relationship to proceed because:

1. The client has adjusted to or is prepared, for a while, to work on the basis of the counsellor's view.
2. The counsellor has adjusted to the client's view (it is interesting here to speculate how often counsellors do this).
3. The client and counsellor have negotiated a new shared conceptualisation of the client's problem which is different from their previous initial attempts at understanding (this is an important but poorly understood topic awaiting future empirical inquiry).

If the counsellor and client cannot come to some sort of shared understanding on this issue, the counsellor may, at this point, refer the client to a counsellor who will offer a conceptualisation of the client's problem more acceptable to the client.

While the client and counsellor now agree on problem definition and conceptualisation, they may still disagree concerning what to do about the problem. Thus, a client and counsellor may agree that the client's problem is depression and have a shared conceptualisation of it but may disagree concerning what is to be done about the problem. The client may wish, for example, to minimise or reduce his or her depression whereas the counsellor may deem it productive for the client to tolerate the depression and not try to reduce it but to use it as an impetus for greater self-understanding.

This latter scenario points to a phenomenon quite common according to Maluccio (1979) in whose study counsellors were more ambitious concerning the kinds of changes they wanted their clients to achieve than were the clients themselves. Maluccio found that when clients in his study terminated counselling they were happier with what they had achieved from counselling than were their counsellors. The latter were dissatisfied that their clients had not achieved a fair measure of personality change, whereas the former were pleased with the changes in symptoms that they had achieved through counselling.

Extrapolating from this research it may be that whilst many clients seek goals which are relatively short term in nature counsellors may see the transient quality of such changes and thus prefer to take a longer-term goals perspective and set goals which help to prevent future client relapse. In any event this is an issue that can again be referred for discussion to the reflection process.

Whilst the emphasis so far has been on client outcome goals, other goals exist during counselling that require discussion. One set of goals is client goals that mediate the achievement of outcome goals (mediating goals). These may refer to changes that the client may exhibit outside the counselling process (external) or inside the process (internal). An example of a mediating external client goal might be for the client to successfully execute certain social skills in real life encounters, the achievement of which may help the client initiate friendships (outcome goal). An example of a mediating internal client goal might be for the client to express successfully feelings of annoyance towards the counsellor which may help the client confront his spouse (outcome goal). In addition to what has been said concerning shared agreement between counsellor and client concerning the latter's outcome goals (a point which also applies to the client's mediating goals), it is important that the client understands the therapeutic relevance of the relationship between the achievement of mediating goals and her outcome goals and commits herself to the achievement of these mediating goals. Without such understanding and commitment, the client may begin to feel that she is being asked to pursue goals that are meaningless to her. In which case referring the matter to the reflection process is once again advocated.

Another set of goals that needs to be considered here concerns the goals that the counsellor sets for him- or herself during the counselling process. This is very frequently related to the goals the counsellor sets for the client. For example, if the counsellor believes it is important for the client to trust her, she may set for herself the goal of being especially accepting of the client's ambivalent feelings. Whereas at a later stage and given sufficient trust, she may endeavour to confront the attitudes that underpin such ambivalence. Thus, the goals that counsellors set for themselves are (or should be) heavily dependent upon their view of the client's position in the change process and effective counsellors are highly responsive to such considerations. This issue is explored by Hutchins (in Dryden, 1989) who encourages counsellors to set goals for their own style of intervention while being mindful of the client's predominant style of dealing with the world.

Whilst I am aware that some readers may object that this represents an overly mechanistic view of counselling and that effective counselling is often a highly intuitive activity, I would like to make the point in reply that intuition refers to sensitive judgements that have become internalised and appear, in highly skilled and experienced hands, effortless. However, at some point, these judgements were made at a conscious level and may even with experienced counsellors become conscious again when threats to the alliance appear.

Before leaving the topic of goals I would like to briefly list several points that need to be borne in mind when exploring goals with clients.

1.  Clients may express goals in vague terms. Here it is important to help them specify them in a form that makes the goals achievable and subject to evaluation.
2.  Clients may express goals that involve changes in other people or life

events (for example, 'I want my mother to change', 'My goal is to have the local council find me better accommodation'). In individual counselling it is important to renegotiate goals so that their achievement falls within the client's power (for example, what is the client going to do differently to encourage her mother to change? What is the client going to do to persuade the council to find her better accommodation?).

3. Clients may express goals that are based on their disturbed feelings, attitudes or behaviour (for example, an anorexic client who wishes to lose more weight). Here it is important to deal with the level of disturbance first before setting concrete goals. It is for this reason that some counsellors prefer not to set goals too early in the counselling process.

4. Clients' goals change during the counselling process and thus counsellors need to update themselves on the current status of their clients' goals during the reflection process. (Some counsellors do this formally in specific review sessions.)

# Tasks

The final component in this tripartite view of the therapeutic alliance pertains to tasks — activities carried out by both counsellor and client which are goal-directed in nature. Such tasks may be broad in nature (for example, engage in the broad task of self-exploration in person-centred counselling) or more specific (engage in a two-chair dialogue in gestalt counselling).

However, when an alliance perspective on tasks is taken, the slant is different from one which emphasises the content of such tasks and several questions become salient.

*Does the client understand the nature of the therapeutic tasks that she is being called upon to execute?*

If the client does not either explicitly or implicitly understand (1) that she has tasks to perform in the counselling process and (2) what these tasks are, then a potential obstacle to the client's progress through the counselling process appears. As with other potential obstacles this may be dealt with by referring the matter for discussion to that part of the counselling dialogue which I have termed 'the reflection process' where counsellor and client step back and discuss what has gone on between them during counselling sessions.

Aware of how important it is for clients to understand their role in the counselling process and more specifically what their tasks are in that process, some counsellors formally attempt to initiate clients into their role at the outset (see Day and Sparacio, in Dryden, 1989).

*If the client understands the nature of the tasks that she is called upon to execute, does she see the instrumental value of carrying out these tasks?*

As noted earlier tasks are best conceptualised as ways of achieving therapeutic goals. Thus a client may understand what her tasks are but may be uncertain how carrying these out may help her to achieve her outcome goals. For example, a client may wish to handle interpersonal conflict in a more constructive way, for example by being assertive with his spouse rather than aggressive. However, he may not see the link between being able to do this and being asked to free associate in the relatively unstructured setting of psychodynamic counselling. Alternatively, another client may not see how disputing her irrational beliefs about competence (as required in cognitive–behavioural counselling) will necessarily help her to overcome her examination anxiety. Thus, from an alliance perspective it is very important that clients be helped to understand the link between carrying out their counselling tasks and achieving their outcome goals. This holds true whether the client's tasks are to be performed within the counselling session or between counselling sessions in their everyday lives.

*Does the client have the ability to carry out the therapeutic tasks required of her?*

The question of ability is important since, although the execution of particular tasks may facilitate client change, if the client is unable to carry out these then this poses a threat to the therapeutic alliance. It may be productive, therefore, for clients to receive specific training in executing their tasks if they are unable to do so at a given point. For example, the client task of disputing irrational beliefs in cognitive–behavioural counselling involves the following client subtasks:

1. Becoming aware of feeling emotionally distressed.
2. Identifying one or more irrational beliefs that underpin such distress.
3. Questioning the irrationality implicit in such beliefs.
4. Answering one's questions in a persuasive way.
5. Replacing one's irrational beliefs with more rational alternatives.
6. Acting on the new rational beliefs.

It is hopefully clear from such a detailed analysis of client task behaviour that the client's ability to successfully execute such a task depends upon (1) how effective the counsellor has been in training the client to do this within the counselling sessions and (2) how much successful practice the client has undertaken both within and between sessions.

It may be the case, however, that a client's lack of personal resources, whether intellectual in nature or attributable to current levels of emotional disturbance, may impede the client's ability to perform a given task. In such cases it is the counsellor's responsibility to modify the task accordingly or ensure that the client is able to carry out a different task more suited to the client's *present* level of ability.

### *Does the client have the confidence to execute the task?*

A similar point can be made here as has been made above. Certain client tasks (and in particular those that clients are asked to execute between sessions – the so-called 'homework assignments') require a certain degree of task confidence on the part of the client if she is to execute it successfully. So the client may understand the nature of the task, see its therapeutic relevance, have the ability to carry it out but may not do so because she predicts that she doesn't have the confidence to do it. Here the counsellor is called upon to help prepare the client in one of two ways. First, the counsellor may need to help the client practise the task in controlled conditions (usually within the counselling session) to the extent that she feels confident to do it on her own. Secondly, the counsellor may encourage the client to carry out the task unconfidently, pointing out that confidence comes from the result of undertaking an activity (i.e. from practice) and is rarely experienced before the activity is first attempted. Counsellors who use analogies within the experience of the client (for example, learning to drive a car) often succeed at helping the client understand this important point.

### *Does the task have sufficient therapeutic potency to facilitate goal achievement?*

If all the aforementioned conditions (i.e. the client understands the nature and therapeutic relevance of task execution, and she has sufficient ability and confidence to perform the task) are met, the client may still not gain therapeutic benefit from undertaking a task because the task does not have sufficient therapeutic potency to help the client achieve her goals. For example, certain client tasks, if sufficiently well carried out, will probably lend to client change. Thus exposing oneself, in vivo or through imagination, to a phobic object will probably yield some therapeutic benefit (Rachman and Wilson, 1980). However, certain tasks may have much less therapeutic potency to achieve a similar result. Thus it has yet to be demonstrated that free association or disputing one's irrational beliefs (in the counselling session rather than in the feared situation, i.e. without exposure) has much therapeutic effect in overcoming phobias. Here then the counsellor's task is to become *au fait* with the current research literature on the subject at hand and not discourage the client by encouraging her to carry out a task which is unlikely, even under the most favourable conditions, to produce much therapeutic benefit.

In this respect there are certain client problems which do seem to call for the execution of specific client tasks. Apart from phobic problems mentioned above, obsessive–compulsive problems seem to call for the client to employ some variant of response prevention in his or her everyday life (Rachman and Wilson, 1980) and problems of depression seem to call for the client to modify distorted thought patterns (Beck et al., 1979) and troublesome elements of their significant interpersonal relationships (Klerman et al., 1984) in order to gain therapeutic benefit. It must be stressed, however, that our current knowledge does not yield detailed therapeutic task-related menus for a wide range of specific client problems and for the most part performing a wide variety of tasks may yield a comparable therapeutic result (Stiles, Shapiro and Elliott, 1986). In which case the issues detailed above become particularly salient.

### Does the client understand the nature of the counsellor's tasks and how these relate to her own?

So far I have focused on issues which deal with clients' tasks. However, in addition to the foregoing, it is important that the client understands (either at an explicit or implicit level) the counsellor's interventions and their rationale. In particular the more the client can understand how her tasks relate to the tasks of her counsellor, the more each can concentrate on effective task execution, the purpose of which, as has been stressed above, is to facilitate the attainment of the client's goals. Should the client be puzzled concerning the counsellor's tasks and how these relate to her own she will be sidetracked from performing her own tasks and begin to question what the counsellor is doing and perhaps even the counsellor's competence. These doubts, if not explored and dealt with in the reflection process, constitute a threat at all levels of the therapeutic alliance. An additional strategy that may prevent the development of client's doubts is for the counsellor to explain, at an appropriate stage in the counselling .process, his tasks and why he is intervening in the way he has chosen to do. This is akin to the use of structuring discussed by Day and Sparacio (in Dryden, 1989) and can be usefully linked to a discussion of the client's complementary tasks.

### Counsellor skill

Until quite recently the issue of counsellors' skill in executing their tasks in the therapeutic process has received little attention in the counselling literature. However, recent investigations (e.g. Luborsky et al., 1985) have brought to light an important and quite obvious point that the skill with which counsellors perform their own tasks in counselling has a positive influence on client outcome. From an alliance perspective, the degree to which clients make progress may be due in some measure to the skilled execution of counsellors' tasks. This means that we must not assume that even well trained counsellors demonstrate equal skill in performing their tasks. A further implication is that skill factors need more prominent attention in counsellor training and supervision than has hitherto been the case. Trainers and supervisors require concrete and detailed evidence concerning how skilfully counsellors have executed their tasks and need to rely less upon counsellors' descriptions of what they did in counselling sessions and more on specific ways of appraising skill (for example, through audio-taped cassette recordings of counselling sessions or at the very least through very detailed process notes).

## Varying the use of counsellors' tasks

A theme that has run through this chapter so far, albeit implicitly, is that since clients vary (along several key dimensions), counsellors need to vary accordingly their own contribution to the counselling process. This point is well made by Hutchins (in Dryden, 1989) who argues that counsellors can improve the relationship they have with their clients by varying the tasks they use with different clients. Whilst he focuses on the client's predominant modes of dealing with the world, he makes the point that counsellors too have similar predominant modes. Whilst in an ideal world, effective counsellors would, with equal facility, be able to use cognitive, behavioural and affective tasks, the fact that counsellors have their own limitations means that it is a temptation for counsellors to restrict themselves to using tasks which reflect their predominant orientation (cognitive, emotive or behavioural). Hutchins's analysis implies that should counsellors restrict themselves to using particular intervention modes (i.e. cognitive, emotive or behavioural), they would help a smaller range of clients than they could help if they became more flexible in freely and appropriately using cognitive, emotive and behavioural tasks. It follows from this that to increase their effectiveness in the task domain of the alliance, counsellors need to acknowledge their own task preferences *and* work on broadening their own range of task behaviour – a task which itself calls for continual exposure to what therapeutic models other than their own preferred model have to offer. This would mean that counsellors of different orientations would learn from each other to a greater extent than is currently the case, a point which would hasten the move towards eclecticism and integration in counselling and psychotherapy, now gathering momentum on both sides of the Atlantic.

# The Three Components of the Therapeutic Alliance are Interrelated

So far I have dealt with the three components of the therapeutic alliance – bonds, goals and tasks – as if they were separate. In reality, however, they are interrelated, and I will bring this chapter to a close by focusing on a few ways in which they do interrelate.

1. Successful structuring of the counsellor's and client's task behaviour in the counselling process can help to strengthen the initial bond between counsellor and client and serve to clarify the client's goals.
2. Skilful responding to a client's early test of trust in the counselling relationship can free the client to engage more deeply in the counselling process, i.e. it will deepen the bond between counsellor and client and enable the client to concentrate on his or her own task behaviour.
3. Sensitive and effective handling of client reluctance will increase the likelihood that the 'reluctant' client will commit himself to the counselling process and set goals that are relevant to himself (rather than to any coercive third party).
4. Specifying and agreeing a client's goals helps to ensure that both counsellor and client are working to the same end, facilitates a working bond, and enables client and counsellor to choose more appropriate tasks to achieve the agreed and specified goals.
5. Selecting tasks that meet a client's predominant pattern of dealing with the world encourages the counsellor to speak the client's 'language' and serves to strengthen the therapeutic bond by helping the client feel understood in the task domain of the alliance.
6. Meeting a client's expectations for counselling early in the relationship helps to establish a solid relationship (bond) into which appropriate challenges (tasks) can be introduced in the middle stages of the work to facilitate client change.
7. Becoming aware and handling sensitively so-called transference phenomena militates against the development of self- and relationship-defeating patterns in the counselling process and helps clients achieve their goals more effectively.
8. Skilful handling of the termination process and the client's attempts to terminate a counselling relationship prematurely, consolidates the client's progress towards goal attainment and helps to bring the bond to a mutually satisfying end.

# References

BECK, A.T., RUSH, A.J., SHAW, B.F. and EMERY, G. (1979). *Cognitive Therapy of Depression*. New York: Guilford.

BEUTLER, L.E., CRAGO, M. and ARIZMENDI, T.G. (1986). Therapist variables in psychotherapy process and outcome. In Garfield, S.L. and Bergin, A.E. (Eds.) *Handbook of Psychotherapy and Behavior Change*, 3rd edn. New York: Wiley.

BORDIN, E.S. (1979). The generalizability of the psychoanalytic concept of the working alliance. *Psychotherapy: Theory, Research and Practice* **16**, 252–260.

CHAPLIN, J. (1988). *Feminist Counselling in Action*. London: Sage.

CLARKSON, P. (1989). *Gestalt Counselling in Action*. London: Sage.

d'ARDENNE, P. and MAHTANI, A. (1989). *Transcultural Counselling in Action*. London: Sage.

DORN, F.J. (Ed.) (1984). *The Social Influence Process in Counseling and Psychotherapy*. Springfield, IL: Charles C. Thomas.

DRYDEN, W. (Ed.) (1989). *Key Issues for Counselling in Action*. London: Sage.

FOREMAN, S.A. and MARMAR, C.R. (1985). Therapist actions that address initially poor therapeutic alliances in psychotherapy. *American Journal of Psychiatry* **142**, 922–926.

JACOBS, M. (1988). *Psychodynamic Counselling in Action*. London: Sage.

KLERMAN, G.L., WEISSMAN, M.M., ROUNSAVILLE, B.J. and CHEVRON, E.S. (1984). *Interpersonal Psychotherapy of Depression*. New York: Basic Books.

LUBORSKY, L., MCLELLAN, A.T., WOODY, G.E., O'BRIEN, C.P. and AUERBACH, A. (1985). Therapist success and its determinants. *Archives of General Psychiatry* **42**, 602–611.

MALUCCIO, A.N. (1979). *Learning from Clients: Interpersonal helping as viewed by clients and social workers*. New York: Free Press.

MEARNS, D. and THORNE, B. (1988). *Person-centred Counselling in Action*. London: Sage.

MORAS, K. and STRUPP, H.H. (1982). Pretherapy interpersonal relations, patients' alliance, and outcome in brief therapy. *Archives of General Psychiatry* **39**, 405–409.

RACHMAN, S.J. and WILSON, G.T. (1980) *The Effects of Psychological Therapy*, 2nd enlarged edn. New York: Pergamon.

STEWART, I. (1989). *Transactional Analysis Counselling in Action*. London: Sage.

STILES, W.B., SHAPIRO, D.A. and ELLIOTT, R. (1986). Are all psychotherapies equivalent? *American Psychologist* **41**(2), 165–180.

TROWER, P., CASEY, A. and DRYDEN, W. (1988). *Cognitive–Behavioural Counselling in Action*. London: Sage.

# Chapter 4
# Therapeutic Alliances in Couple Counselling I Pre-counselling Influences

Whilst there are different theoretical perspectives on couple counselling, the effectiveness of all approaches to couple work depends on the establishment and maintenance of a sound working relationship between counsellor and clients. In this and the following chapter I wish to focus on therapeutic alliances as they pertain to the practice of couple counselling, and to consider some of the issues that emerge from taking this perspective. In the present chapter, I will consider the concept of the therapeutic alliance and explore the pre-counselling influences that are exerted on the development and maintenance of therapeutic alliances in couple counselling. In the following chapter I will focus on matters pertaining to these alliances as they unfold during the counselling process.

The practice of couple counselling involves the counsellor attending to a complex set of alliances with a number of client systems. Barker (1984) has argued that the couple counsellor has to be mindful of serving at least seven different client systems: (1) the couple dyad; (2) the woman as an individual; (3) the man as an individual; (4) those dependent on the couple; (5) society; (6) the authority that sanctions the work of the couple counsellor; and (7) the counsellor him- or herself.

What does it mean to have a therapeutic alliance with the couple dyad? Harper (1981) considers that the couple is an abstraction and that it is nonsensical for counsellors to have a therapeutic alliance with an abstraction. Gurman (1981a) disagrees and notes:

While the couple does not, of course, have a palpable organismic existence as a psychological entity apart from the separate existence of each partner, they do share a behavioral and dynamic relatedness which must be considered functionally in its own right. Thus the therapist must identify early the unspoken language, implicit agreements, and unconscious contracts . . . which simultaneously bond the partners

---

First published in 1985 with Patricia Hunt.

together and create the medium for the emergence of the current continuing conflict. (p. 85)

Most couple counsellors would probably concur with Gurman's view and would consider that the alliance they are most concerned with in couple counselling is that with the dyad. However, there are six other systems to consider and there *may* be times when the basic desires of these other systems conflict with those of the couple system.

First, there may be occasions when the interests of the relationship conflict with the interest of one of the individual partners. For example, a woman may wish to pursue a career which threatens her partner. If she takes this course of action she may jeopardize her relationship, whereas if she does not she remains unfulfilled in a significant area of her life.

Secondly, there may be situations when the interests of those dependent on the couple are not served if the couple pursue their interests. Thus, a couple may agree that the best way to bring up their children is to subject them to frequent beatings to teach them a lesson. The children will thus suffer if the couple put their values into practice.

Thirdly, society's interests may be threatened by the couple pursuing their interests. Thus, a couple may preserve that relationship by pursuing a 'career' in drug trafficking. The risks to members of society are obvious if they do so, whereas, if they do not, their relationship may dissolve.

Fourthly, couple counsellors have to be mindful of the views of their sanctioning authority which may conflict with the wishes of the couple. The counsellor may work in an agency which regards divorce as 'sinful'. How, then, does such a counsellor respond to a couple who mutually agree to divorce?

Finally, the values of the couple may seriously conflict with those of the counsellor. The couple may support the views and causes of the National Front and seek help from a counsellor who finds these values abhorrent.

In all these situations the couple counsellor's interventions are going to be coloured by his or her decision concerning which system to give priority to at any point in time. The practice of couple counselling cannot therefore be a value-free exercise and is likely to often pose searching dilemmas for its practitioners (Dryden, 1985).

# The Concept of the Therapeutic Alliance

The concept of the therapeutic alliance was first employed in the psychoanalytical literature, although in recent years it has been used to consider the complex of attachments and shared understandings formed and activities undertaken by counsellors and clients as the former attempt to help the latter with their personal problems. In psychodynamic psychotherapy, the therapeutic alliance has been used to refer to the non-transferential or more rational aspects of the therapeutic relationship. Sterba (1934) was one of the first to write of an ego-level identification with and positive attitude towards the therapist which helped the patient to work towards the accomplishment of common therapeutic tasks. Since then the concept has been considered from a variety of different perspectives, which has led to a situation of conceptual confusion. For example, while most writers make the two-part distinction between the therapeutic alliance and the transference relationship, Greenson (1967) and Weiner (1975) refer to three aspects: (1) the real relationship, (2) the working alliance and (3) transference.

The theoretical work of Bordin (1979) has done much to elevate the 'therapeutic alliance' to a position of greater conceptual clarity and we shall draw heavily upon his work in both this chapter and the next. As I saw in Chapter 3, Bordin argued that the therapeutic alliance is made up of three major components: (1) bonds, (2) goals and (3) tasks. Summarising his views, the *bonds* refer to the quality of the relationship between the participants, the *goals* are the ends of the therapeutic journey, whilst the *tasks* are the means for achieving these ends. Disruption to the therapeutic journey might occur because the 'travellers' (1) do not get on or have a relationship which is not conducive to the goals or tasks of therapy (weak or inappropriate bonding); (2) disagree on journey's end (non-agreement about goals); and/or (3) prefer different ways of reaching the therapeutic destination (non-agreement about tasks). These three components as they pertain to the practice of couple counselling will be considered separately in greater detail in the following chapter.

It is important to note that both the counsellor and clients make contributions to the development and maintenance of therapeutic alliances in couple counselling. Failure to develop sound alliances, then, may be due to counsellor factors, client factors or both sets of factors as they interact with each other. For example, a counsellor may be poorly skilled in the technical aspects of the practice of couple work, the clients may not be capable of meeting the demands of the particular type of couple counselling being offered (Hartley and Strupp, 1983) or clients and counsellor may seek to form a different type of relationship with one another. In addition, agency factors (the setting in which therapy takes place) play their part in this interaction. When failure in couple counselling occurs, it is important to scan the complex set of contributions made by participants, and their interaction with each other and with the agency on each of the three components of the alliance, to gain a full understanding of the failure.

Some research studies have shown that when counsellors in individual work pay attention to alliance-related problems and intervene accordingly, then poor outcome can be avoided. For example Lansford (quoted in

Bordin, 1983) found that counsellors' sensitivity to weakening of the alliance and their effectiveness in repairing those 'breaks' were positively correlated with a good therapeutic outcome. Furthermore, Lehrke (1978) found that a counsellor's failure to respond, except by listening, to clients' expressions of interest or concern regarding alliance-related issues was predictive of alliance failure. These findings echo Hartley's (1978) view that 'in individual therapy problems in the alliance take precedence over all others; the therapist must recognize them and intervene before further progress can be made' (p. 8). Thus, while threats to the alliance may come from each of the partipants' contributions or their interaction, it is incumbent upon the counsellor to intervene accordingly. Failure to do so augurs poorly for therapeutic outcome. Whether this conclusion applies to couple counselling awaits further inquiry.

Finally, there are probably different types of helping alliances. Luborsky (1976) distinguished between an alliance in which the client experiences the counsellor as supportive and helpful, with himself as the recipient, and one where a sense of collaboration is developed between counsellor and client, where both join forces and work together in a joint struggle against what is impeding the client. In the latter type, the client is more of an active participant in the therapeutic process, whereas he is more passive in the former. Luborsky's work was based on individual counselling, and it remains to be seen whether the same two helping alliances emerge in couple counselling or whether other types are reliably found in this counselling arena. Additional research is required to determine whether particular types of alliance endure throughout the course of couple counselling or whether particular types become salient at different times for different couples.

# Pre-counselling Factors affecting Therapeutic Alliances in Couple Counselling

The practice of couple counselling takes place neither in a vacuum nor in isolation from what the couple and the counsellor bring to the endeavour. In the rest of this chapter I will focus on factors that influence the development and maintenance of the therapeutic alliances in couple counselling before the couple even meet their counsellor. First, I shall cover the contributions that the couple are likely to bring to counselling which have an influence on the set of therapeutic alliances. Then, I shall outline the counsellor's contributions. Finally, I shall consider how the agency in which couple counselling takes place plays its part in framing counselling and how such factors may affect the alliances that emerge and are sustained in such work.

## Couple factors

The ways in which couples define their problems and the processes by which they decide to seek help both have an important effect on the way therapeutic alliances may develop. If we consider problem definition, couples may seek help after arriving at a mutually agreed definition of their relationship problems to which they both contribute. This situation is the couple counsellor's dream in that the couple's definition of their problems is congruent with the way that the counsellor is likely to define their concerns and thus the latter is likely to have few problems in moving from problem definition to problem assessment. Alternatively the woman, for example, may consider that the couple have problems to which they both contribute whereas the man's view may be that his partner is 'sick' or that her unreasonable behaviour has led to tension between them and that her actions are due to hormonal changes associated with the menopause. In this scenario, the danger is that since the woman's definition of their problem is probably more congruent with the counsellor's definition than is her partner's, the counsellor may more easily form an alliance with the woman than with the man. In so doing the counsellor may alienate the man, further entrenching him in his definition of their problems.

The way the couple decide to seek help is also of relevance when alliances are studied in couple counselling. Hunt (1984) in her research on clients' reactions to marriage guidance counselling found that for 50 per cent of her sample it was a particular event that triggered them to seek help. 'For the other 50 percent ... the trigger event was hard to define and contact seemed more to be a response to mounting pressure and an inability to make a decision, or to an accumulation of stress that was perhaps affecting their health' (p. 74). Whilst there is no research which deals with the question concerning the effect of specific or non-specific problem triggers on the development and maintenance of couple counselling alliances, some speculation is in order. It may be more difficult for couple counsellors to shift the focus of exploration from overt to underlying issues in cases where specific triggers have prompted the couple to seek help for their difficulties than in cases where less specific triggers exist.

Garvin and Seabury (1984) also note that the events leading to couples applying for help have implications for their view of clienthood and their expectations of the role of their helpers. A crisis may encourage the couple to enter couple counselling with productive views about clienthood or it may lead them to expect instant help from the counsellor who at the same time may be prepared for a long-sustained period of on-going counselling. In the latter situation the resulting discrepancy threatens the couple counselling alliances between couple and counsellor at the outset of the work.

Another pertinent issue concerning a couple's decision to seek help for their relationship problems relates to the extent to which both partners have applied for help voluntarily. It often happens that one partner willingly seeks help while dragging the reluctant partner with him or her (metaphorically and occasionally literally!). The threat to the three-person alliance is ever present as long as one partner feels coerced to participate in the couple counselling process. When both partners are seeking help voluntarily then this augurs well for the development and maintenance of the various alliances between the participants. Occasionally, both partners seek help involuntarily. They may have been recommended such help by an authority and perceived the suggestion as an order, or they have been referred to a couple counselling agency by a helping professional who has previously failed to help them. In such instances, the skills of couple counsellors to avoid unproductive alliances with reluctant couples are severely tested. Indeed, sometimes it would be an error to offer couple counselling help to such clients.

When a couple decides to seek help from a couple counsellor they bring to this enterprise general attitudes towards seeking help and specific attitudes towards seeking couple counselling in particular. These attitudes may be well developed and easily verbalised or they may be vaguely defined and not available to the person's awareness. In the latter cases such attitudes may be inferred from the person's behaviour, although this, of course, is a hazardous enterprise.

General attitudes to seeking help are productive when the person can freely admit to having problems, believes that seeking help is a legitimate activity, not a source of shame or embarrassment, and brings a healthy scepticism to what the counsellor has to offer. The person is able to take what is helpful from the counselling process and reject what is unhelpful without losing respect for the counsellor. Examples of unproductive attitudes to seeking help are demonstrated when the person assumes an overly dependent stance in therapy or when the person's sense of autonomy is easily threatened by the act of applying for help. In the former case, the person is likely not to utilise his or her own potential for solving problems and will look to the counsellor as the sole source of help. The person is likely to ask the counsellor frequently what he or she should do and remain in counselling for a long time rather than use it as an opportunity to develop resources and skills which are then applied to his or her everyday relationship experiences. In the latter case, the person brings a compulsive self-reliance to counselling and tends to deny that problems exist, or that they are as bad as they are, or that he or she is unable to cope with them. The person may attempt to call into question the counsellor's qualifications as a helper or his or her ability to provide effective assistance. It is important to reiterate that these are attitudes to help that such persons *bring with them* to the counselling enterprise. While these attitudes may be less problematic in couple than in individual counselling (given that there is less scope in the former for intense attachments between clients and counsellor), they do exert an important influence on the type of alliances that develop in couple counselling. When the counsellor is faced with a situation where both partners have unproductive attitudes towards help, then again their skills to develop appropriate and helpful alliances are severely tested. When one partner has a productive attitude to help whilst the other has an unproductive attitude, the danger exists that the couple counsellor will ally himself with the former and thus further alienate the latter.

Couples' specific attitudes to couple counselling depend heavily on their expectations of this form of help. Duckro, Beal and George (1979) have made the telling point that it is important to distinguish between anticipations and preferences when considering these expectations. Couples may correctly anticipate what might happen in couple counselling but prefer a different kind of process. Frequently couples do not have clear anticipations of what couple counselling will be like (Brannen and Collard, 1982; Hunt, 1985). Barker (1984) has argued that this is because (1) couple counselling has a vague public image, and (2) there is so much variation in the way couple counsellors work. Brannen and Collard (1982) further speculate that this may be so because clients are so preoccupied with their painful feelings that this may interfere with their thinking about their anticipations.

Research carried out on clients' expectations of couple counselling has been problematic for two reasons. First, such studies (Brannen and Collard, 1982; Hunt, 1985) have tried to ascertain what clients expected to receive from couple counselling *after* they have been exposed to such help; thus experience has probably coloured their responses. Secondly, these studies fail to make the important distinction mentioned above between clients' anticipations of and preferences for couple counselling. Whilst Brannen and Collard's and Hunt's data show that clients seeking help from Relate and a hospital-based couple counselling agency had unclear anticipations concerning what would actually occur, their findings indicate that clients' preferences for what they hoped to receive were better formed although quite diverse. Data from Relate clients show that their preferences for help range from independent, unbiased commentaries on their relationship, to help in tracing missing partners, to advice on specific topics (Heisler, 1980; Hunt, 1985). Brannen and Collard (1982) and Hunt (1985) also refer to the tacit widespread assumption among clients that Relate is a 'mending service'. One of Hunt's interviewees said in this regard:

> It might be a wrong assumption on my part but I assumed that if you set up marriage guidance it must be basically to try and help couples stay together ... Well I don't think either of us would have gone there unless we wanted to. I can't see that anyone would go to marriage guidance if they didn't want to save their marriage.

Thus a good proportion of Relate clients hope that it will provide advice on helping them stay partnered, whereas counsellors are largely non-directive and generally refrain from giving advice and do not as a matter of course share the assumption that their first priority is to help clients mend their relationships. These discrepancies if unmodified remain threats to the therapeutic alliances in couple counselling. Not only do some clients drop out from Relate counselling when their preferences are not met, but other clients remain in the hope that if they are 'good clients' such advice may be eventually given to them (Hunt, 1985). The fact that the agency still has 'Marriage Guidance' in its title may be partly responsible for the perpetuation of the widespread assumption that advice will be provided (Keithley, 1982), given that clients often confuse the terms guidance and advice.

There is some research evidence to suggest that men are more likely to prefer more directive help and advice from their Relate counsellors than women, who tend to prefer a more non-directive, reflective style of help (Brannen and Collard, 1982). Hunt (1984) found a small trend in this direction but noted that men who were willing to stay in counselling for a while, and thereby learned how to use a less directive form of help, were more satisfied with the process than Brannen and Collard's (1982) male respondents. These data, although retrospective, would suggest that the working alliance in the task realm between Relate counsellors and women may be stronger at the outset of counselling than between counsellors and men.

Another area worthy of study and having implications for the development and maintenance of therapeutic alliances in couple work concerns the anticipations of and preferences for help among clients of different social classes. There is some evidence that lower-class persons are more likely to prefer their counsellors to be active and to give advice than middle-class persons (Overall and Aronson, 1963; Mayer and Timms, 1970; Lazare, Eisenthal and Wasserman, 1975; Irwin, 1980). These preferences may make it more difficult for Relate counsellors to form productive alliances with their lower-class clients since these helpers (who are predominantly middle-class women) are likely to favour a more non-directive form of help. It is probable that clients' preferences for particular forms of help in couple counselling are closely linked to the problem-solving styles that these clients typically employ in their everyday experiences (Maluccio, 1979). Thus, those men who employ an active, behavioural-focused style of problem-solving in their lives may prefer the same style of approach in couple counselling. This remains a fruitful area for future empirical inquiry.

Couples' views about couple counselling may be further influenced by their experiences of the referral process, although Brannen and Collard (1982) found that referral agents rarely give precise information concerning what help couples can realistically anticipate from couple counselling agencies. However, couples do place interpretations on what referral agents say even if the latter do not give precise information, and these interpretations have relevance for the type of couple counselling alliances couples anticipate. I once saw a young couple in a marriage guidance setting who were quite distressed by their GP's suggestion that they seek help from their local Relate agency for the wife's dyspareunia (pain on sexual intercourse). Although the doctor explained that Relate had a special sex counselling programme, the couple were upset because they thought that the doctor had spotted some hidden relationship problem that they were not aware of, since they believed that Relate was 'the place to go if you had relationship (as opposed to sexual) problems'. Furthermore, the husband anticipated that treatment would take place in a group setting and had been quite anxious about this prior to their appointment.

The final set of client factors to be considered in relation to the types of alliances that are likely to emerge in couple counselling concerns the personal resources and personal motives that partners bring with them to the counselling enterprise. Concerning clients' resources, a recurrent finding in the counselling outcome literature is that clients who benefit most from counselling are those who need it least, i.e. those who already have strong personal resources. Moras and Strupp (1982) found that clients in individual counselling who formed collaborative and positively toned alliances with their counsellors were those who were judged to have already basically adequate interpersonal relationships prior to embarking on counselling. Their positively toned involvement in counselling was more productive of good outcome than counsellor technique and those therapeutic relationship factors that are commonly believed to be primary agents of change. If this finding is replicated in couple counselling it means that the strength of the alliance between counsellor and clients is to some degree predetermined by what clients bring to the counselling process. If one member of the couple has had a history of adequate interpersonal relationships and the other partner has not, the counsellor may well find it easier to develop a sound alliance with the former, thus again possibly further alienating the latter.

A number of writers on couple counselling have considered the various personal motives partners bring to the therapeutic process. Whilst much of this work is derived from clinical experience rather than empirical research, it is likely that these motives have already been formed prior to partners entering counselling. Indeed, these writers argue that such motives and the counselling roles that partners develop based on them are designed to elicit responses from counsellors that confirm partners' implicit or explicit *pre-counselling* ideas about their relationship, who is to blame for the couple's distress and whether they want their relationship to continue or not.

Smith and Grunebaum (1976) and Broderick (1983) have written on the motivations and consequent roles brought by partners to the counselling situation that are likely to sabotage the establishment of working alliances in couple counselling. It is important to reiterate at the outset that partners rarely disclose these motives spontaneously. They are either available to the partner's awareness but not disclosed or are outside that person's awareness. These motivations have also been described as 'hidden agendas' (Irwin, 1980). The most common motivations are the following.

### 'I want out'

Here one or both partners come to couple counselling with a strong investment for it to be unsuccessful and thus seek to avoid developing a lasting alliance with the counsellor. They can then say, 'Our relationship is hopeless, look even counselling was of no help', and start the disengagement process with a minimum of guilt. Some of these partners can actually 'appear' to be 'model' clients and the counsellor may leave the first few counselling sessions highly encouraged about the prospects of an effective outcome. Then the partner who is 'looking for an exit' (Smith and Grunebaum, 1976) will cancel or fail to attend further appointments much to the puzzlement of both the counsellor and the spouse who is left abandoned in the hands of the counsellor. Other partners who 'want out' are highly negative in their attitude at the outset of counselling, and may demonstrate this by attacking the counsellor overtly or by covertly undermining his or her attempts to establish triangular rapport.

### 'Could you live with him (or her)?'

Here one or both partners consider that they are on the receiving end of the partner's unreasonable behaviour and that their own conduct is either exemplary or only poor because they have to put up with such unfair treatment. These partners seek to get the counsellor on his or her side either by asking direct questions such as 'would *you* put up with it?' or by making similar appeals non-verbally. They will direct most of their remarks to the counsellor and resist attempts to speak directly to the partner. If asked to reflect on their own contribution to the couple distress they will bring up further evidence of the partner's unfair treatment. Some partners who enter counselling with this motivation attempt to play the role of the counsellor's ally, joining forces with the counsellor to help the 'sick' or 'bad' spouse.

### 'Help me to stay married – I'm sick'

This motivation is held by those partners whose spouses have left them or are on the brink of leaving them. Often this is in response to the first partner's newly discovered affair or long-standing drink problem. Such spouses who are seeking the 'sick' label may try to convince both the counsellor and their partner that their behaviour is out of their control or due to severe intrapsychic problems. They seek to be pitied rather than blamed because they consider that guilt or compassion will stop their partner from abandoning them. In doing so they tend to praise the spouse, whom they consider to be a wonderful person, 'for putting up with a wretch like me'. This self-damning attitude is phony and as soon as these clients obtain their objective they leave counselling. They promise to be 'good hard-working clients' but rarely are. Similar to this pattern is one best called 'I'll change, I really will'. Here the person is not seeking a sick role but admits to causing the relationship distress and promises to be different in the future. This enthusiasm is often not backed up with real attempts to change. The motive is once again to save their relationship and return to the status quo.

### 'It's her hormones (his mid-life crisis)'

In this scenario, one partner comes to counselling believing that he or she is blameless and that the partner's dissatisfaction with the relationship is due to 'a phase he or she is going through'. These partners either deny that there is anything wrong with their relationship from their perspective, or admit that there is couple discord but insist that this is caused by the problems of the partner which are due to the normal stresses of ageing such as the menopause or the mid-life crisis. They strongly resist considering that they may play a part in the couple discord and, if they remain in counselling, strive to avoid self-observation (Smith and Grunebaum, 1976). Another version of this motivation is displayed by partners who say, 'Ours isn't a perfect relationship, but whose is nowadays?'

### 'I'll make someone pay for this'

Sometimes one partner issues the other an ultimatum: 'Come to couple counselling or I'll leave you.' Occasionally, particularly in my experience, in the case of men, this can be the stimulus for productive involvement in counselling. More frequently, however, the partner resents being placed in an ultimatum situation, and responds by adopting a difficult role in the counselling process. Such partners may challenge the counsellor for control of the session, sabotage the alliances that the counsellor seeks to establish with both of them and adopt other blocking tactics. Basically the partner feels trapped and seeks to make someone pay for his or her plight.

Whilst couple counsellors of different persuasions will choose to respond to these threats to the therapeutic alliances in different ways, it is clear that, unless these 'hidden agendas' are dealt with in some way, effective couple counselling will in these circumstances rarely take place.

Having reviewed some of the pre-counselling couple factors that influence the ways in which in couple counselling alliances develop and are sustained, I will now consider counsellor factors.

## Counsellor factors

Couple counsellors bring to their work a host of factors which may affect the alliances that emerge during counselling.

With respect to the personal qualities of couple counsellors, Broderick (1983) in an informal survey noted that his own pool of (American) trainees over many years had personality profiles that were very similar to those of couple counselling clients. Both were different from the average person in the street and from individual counselling clients. Summarising these profiles, he wrote that couple counsellors tend to have:

> (1) a high level of interpersonal needs or dependency (this person is sensitive to people and their approval and has a greater than average need for strokes from significant others); (2) a resentment of authority and restrictive social rules; (3) a history of hurts received in intimate relationships starting in childhood; (4) a tendency to utilize the defense mechanisms of denial, that is, putting a good face on things as a means of dealing with problems. (p. 170)

It is important to note that this list of qualities has been derived from informal research on American couple counsellors and needs to be more formally replicated in the UK. However, Broderick's list is surprisingly similar in certain respects to Ellis's (1983) list of the irrational beliefs which may be held by couple counsellors more frequently than one would ideally expect from helping professionals.

1. 'I have to be successful with all of my couple counselling clients practically all of the time!'
2. 'I must be an outstanding couple counsellor, clearly better than other couple counsellors I know or hear about.'
3. 'I have to be greatly respected and loved by all my couple counselling clients.'
4. 'Since I am doing my best and working so hard as a couple counsellor, my clients should be equally hard working and responsible, should listen to me carefully and should always push themselves to change.'
5. 'Because I am a person in my own right, I must be able to enjoy myself during couple counselling sessions and to use these sessions to solve my personal problems as much as to help clients with their difficulties.'

How might these qualities and beliefs affect couple counselling alliances? A couple counsellor's need for approval may distract him or her from the tasks of couple counselling, particularly if couples find them painful or onerous. Such counsellors' prime concern is to keep couples happy; they are often highly regarded by their clients but tend to keep couples in counselling for a long time and to collude with them in avoiding the exploration of painful and difficult issues. In the latter respect, utilisation of the defence mechanism of denial aids this collusive process. Resenting authority and restrictive social rules, some couple counsellors may have ambivalent feelings about the traditional institution of marriage and thus give undue weight to different alternative life-styles. This attitude may lead such counsellors to abuse their traditional therapeutic role in ways suggested by Ellis. Having a history of childhood hurts may lead some couple counsellors to use the arena of couple counselling as an opportunity to work out their childhood problems in a setting which resembles the nuclear family. Object-relations theory would hypothesise that for this to happen such couple counsellors would first have to recreate the circumstances of these hurts in order for them to be resolved. Thus, counsellors may seek unconsciously to achieve bonds similar to those that were formed with their parents in childhood. These 'countertransference' issues are well documented in the therapeutic literature and may be more prevalent in couple counselling given the similarity between this setting and that of the nuclear family. The needs of couple counsellors to be competent and successful may lead them to be intolerant of their clients when the latter fail to improve or fail to carry out suggested homework tasks. Such counsellors would tend to blame couples for the therapeutic impasses that result, instead of acknowledging their own contribution to the resistance, since were they to admit such responsibility they would condemn themselves.

It is important to stress that the aforementioned qualities and beliefs do not inevitably lead to the above problems in couple counselling alliances, but the potential for such disruption is present given their existence. It is to be hoped that couple counsellors are in an on-going supervisory relationship where these tendencies can be discussed so that harm can be minimised in circumstances where counsellor and couple characteristics interact in such a way for these tendencies to become overtly expressed.

Another set of factors which may influence the complex set of therapeutic alliances in couple work concerns the values of the counsellor. Counsellors who prioritise the desires of the couple system above those of each of the individuals in that system are likely to focus most of their counselling attention on the counsellor–couple alliance. Conversely, workers who put the individuals before the couple may well attend first and foremost to the counsellor–female/counsellor–male alliances. Couple counsellors who believe that relationships should be preserved at all costs and construe their role as intervening against this backdrop are likely to form very different alliances from those who believe that their major role is to facilitate (but not influence) the couple's decision to remain partnered or to separate. Surprisingly there is no research which links couple counsellors' values with the formation and maintenance of couple counselling alliances. However, I once rated all the interventions made by a couple counsellor during his work with a couple. This counsellor was selected because he saw his major alliance responsibility was to the couple rather than to the individuals involved. The case was selected by the counsellor as being a good example of the strength of the counsellor–couple alliance. In fact 70 per cent of the counsellor's interventions were addressed to the wife with the remaining 30 per cent being evenly distributed between the 'couple' and the husband. At face value one might conclude in this case that the counsellor–wife alliance was strongest in the alliance matrix, yet since there is a difference between objective and subjective measures of alliances in couple counselling, any research programme studying the relationship between counsellors' values and couple counselling alliances needs to employ both sets of measures. There is some speculation that objective alliance measures would not be good predictions of this relationship. For example, McDonald (1975) notes:

> A strong possibility in the therapeutic situation is the likelihood that a therapist will respond more readily and empathetically to one partner who more nearly represents the therapist's value system. The reverse is also possible, such that the therapist may attempt to compensate for this overidentification by isolation of that person with whom he identifies. (p. 146)

This 'increased attention–decreased attention (through compensation)' pattern may occur on other variables such as counsellor–partner gender, race and class matching. Couple counsellors would do well to observe deviations from their habitual modes of responding in the counselling process and reflect on the meaning of these deviations. In summary, as Coyne and Widiger (1978) and Hadley and Hadley (1976) have warned, couple counsellors need to guard against any tendency to project their reformist values, sex-role expectations and life-style preferences onto their clients. To what extent they can do this remains a matter for private reflection and detailed supervision.

Another influence on the alliance matrix in couple counselling is particularly relevant for those counsellors who have a strong background in individual work and have a history of working with disturbed individuals. Gurman (1981b) has noted that the counsellor may become so intrigued by the psychopathology of one partner that he or she may imply that this person is the 'sick' one. This may result in the counsellor non-therapeutically avoiding the second partner's problems or in that partner feeling excluded from the special alliance that has developed between the counsellor and the 'sick' partner. Gurman argues that counsellors who have been initially trained to view clinical matters from an interpersonal perspective are less likely to fall into this trap of developing special alliances than are those counsellors whose initial training was intrapsychically oriented. Again this is a matter for research.

As shown above, a further counsellor factor influencing couple counselling alliances concerns the therapeutic orientation of the counsellor. Couple counsellors have different approaches to couple work. It is likely that even counsellors who take an eclectic approach to such work are guided by specific principles so that eclectic couple counsellors will differ from each other. In terms of the couple counselling alliances, the various approaches to couple work advocate different therapeutic bonds, suggest different levels of therapeutic goals and demand that different therapeutic tasks are carried out by both counsellors and couples. As will be explored in the following chapter, strong therapeutic alliances will be forged between counsellor and clients when the participants involved form mutually compatible bonds, have a shared understanding of the couple's goals and are able to perform their mutual tasks in the service of achieving these goals. These alliances can be weakened to the extent that there are mismatches on any of these three dimensions. The point of relevance here is that counsellors are limited by the perspective on couple counselling that they bring to this work, and that threats to the development and maintenance of therapeutic alliances in couple work can be explained, in part, by the therapeutic orientation variable.

Couple counsellors differ in the level of therapeutic skill and expertise that they bring to couple work and, even if their clients share their perspectives on alliance-related issues, threats to these alliances may still be present because counsellors may poorly handle bond, goal and task-related interventions.

It is often asked what effect the couple counsellor's gender, age and marital status has on the couple counselling alliances. There is little research evidence to show that these factors have any discernible or reliable impact on these alliances but undoubtedly they do have some impact on certain couples. Broderick (1983) has put this point well. 'I have ... known a number of members of Catholic religious orders, several homosexuals and a number of other never-married people who were top notch [marital] therapists by any measure' (p. 176).

In conclusion, it is important to reiterate that the foregoing factors may interact with the couple factors outlined in the previous section for better or worse with respect to the couple counselling alliances.

## Agency factors

The agency's response to the couple's application for help is also important in facilitating or hindering the development and maintenance of couple counselling alliances as well as in influencing the type of alliances that may be fostered. First, the speed of the agency's response is an important factor.

If there is a long period between the couple's first application and their first counselling session or initial interview, couple counselling may get off to a bad start in that the couple's first experience of the agency has been a negative one. It should be borne in mind in this regard that what constitutes a 'long' and thus unhelpful waiting period is subjectively experienced rather than objectively determined. Secondly, the kind of initial response from the agency is influential mainly in determining what types of therapeutic alliances are favoured in the agency. Writing about psychiatric outpatient clinics (but with direct implications for couple counselling services), Levinson, Merrifield and Berg (1967) have outlined four models of agency response to persons applying for their services before formal counselling begins.

### The diagnostic model

Here the couple submit themselves to a rigorous diagnostic examination of their problems and personalities hoping that it will somehow help them to overcome their difficulties. The counsellor offers treatment on the basis of the couple's (diagnosed) need, not on the basis of their feelings and preferences.

In this model, the couple has begun to be socialised into a therapeutic alliance where their counsellor knows best and where his expertise carries more weight than their desires and notions.

### The suitability model

Here the agency staff select couples deemed to be most qualified to accept and sustain the client role, much as applicants are selected for college, business or government positions.

In this model the agency has clear and firm ideas about the type of couple counselling they are able to offer and which couples can best utilise such services. Couples who are deemed unable, or find it very difficult, to contribute productively to the types of therapeutic alliance implicit in that form of counselling are turned away or referred elsewhere (if there are other agencies offering different forms of couple counselling). Such an agency is likely to have a good record of successful outcomes (since only 'suitable' couples are offered counselling) but this may be misleading if judged independently of the numbers of couples turned away. In this model the couple are also seen as passive recipients of an agency-managed activity – in this case selection rather than diagnosis. Again the couple are not seen as having capacity for affecting the course of their applicancy. They are deemed either as suitable for the predetermined therapeutic programme and thereby accepted, or as unsuitable for the counselling approach on offer and thereby rejected.

## The help-seeking applicant model

Here the burden of decision-making is passed to the couple. The agency adopts a take-it-or-leave-it attitude after their services are explained.

The success of this model depends upon (1) the clear and detailed exposition of the counselling services on offer to enable the couple to make an informed decision, (2) the ability of the couple to make an informed decision at the time and (3) the availability of alternative resources. This latter point is important. If there are no actual or perceived credible alternative counselling services in the community, the couple may decide to accept the offer of help, not because they believe that they can make productive use of it but because they believe they have no other options. This may lead the counsellor to overestimate the extent to which he will be able to develop productive therapeutic alliances with the couple and thus the helper may be less alert to signs that there are problems in the alliance matrix. As Levinson, Merrifield and Berg (1967) note: 'the help-seeking applicant model is insufficient in itself; it takes no account of the appropriateness of the application, the agent's part in the process, the prerogative of the clinic to ultimately offer or withhold treatment, and the multiple priorities and practical problems of treatment allocation in the clinical facility' (p. 403). In short, what is missing from this model is any real transaction between the couple and the agency.

## The negotiated consensus model

Here the agency and the couple engage in a process of negotiation where each takes seriously the views of the other. They try jointly and cooperatively to reach a consensus in their understanding of the couple's problems and in their decision about how these problems are going to be tackled.

In this model a process of negotiation is established and the couple are shown that their views are taken seriously. This open dialogue is central to a frank discussion of matters pertaining to the development and maintenance of productive therapeutic alliances between the partners involved. It is particularly important for the participants to keep this channel of communication open when alliances are threatened so that facilitative repair work of alliance breaks can be achieved (a point which will be underscored in the following chapter).

It is my view that in couple counselling agencies which adopt a policy of negotiated consensus with their applicants counsellors are likely to be more successful in developing and maintaining productive alliances suitable to particular couples than counsellors working in agencies that have different policies. This, of course, awaits empirical inquiry. However, it should be noted that this model may match or be discrepant from how couples anticipate being received by the agency they approach. Some couples, for example, may anticipate and prefer an agency which operates a diagnostic system and definitely not prefer an agency which favours the negotiated consensus model.

Another way in which agency factors can affect the couple counselling alliances concerns the house-style of counselling advocated by the agency. Thus, the house-style of Relate has up to very recently been an amalgam of client-centred counselling and object-relations therapy. Here the emphasis is on exploration, talking and understanding, processes which seem to more closely approximate to women's preferences for counselling (Brannen and Collard, 1982). A focus on action-oriented counselling methods has been introduced into Relate's training curriculum and this development may be more congruent with men's preferences. This latter conclusion stems from the finding that the approach adopted by counsellors in the hospital couple counselling service studied by Brannen and Collard (1982) had a more goal-oriented focus and a more professional ambience than Relate. These factors provided a closer approximation to men's preferences for counselling. As long as couple counselling agencies are going to favour a particular house-style of counselling they had better accept the possibility that they will find it difficult to engage a large minority of their clientèle. As a corrective measure there appears to be a pressing need for an agency in the UK which can offer potential clients a wider range of couple counselling services than is the case at present.

## Preparing couples for couple counselling

Are there any productive steps that agencies and counsellors can take to prepare better couples for couple counselling before the formal process of counselling begins? Such a question is perhaps most pertinent for counsellors who work in agencies which adhere to a help-seeking applicant model where the couple are given an explanation of the services being offered before they are asked to choose whether or not they are going to avail themselves of these services. However, the question is also an apt one for counsellors working in agencies operating different models of responding to clients.

There have been a number of research studies investigating the effectiveness of techniques of systematically preparing clients for counselling, the results of which have been encouraging (Macaskill and Macaskill, 1983). However, only one of these studies (Gaunt, 1981) has focused on the couple counselling modality and further research in this area is called for.

Macaskill and Macaskill (1983) suggest that the aims of systematically preparing couples for couple counselling are to (1) provide couples with an easily understood rationale for this approach and the range of problems for which it is indicated, (2) explain important theoretical concepts central to the approach offered, (3) describe the respective roles of counsellor and clients that have been found to be helpful in the therapeutic approach being outlined, (4) detail the potential difficulties in couple counselling so that the couple can be appropriately forewarned, and (5) suggest reasonable expectations for the outcome of couple counselling.

A number of methods has been used to achieve these aims. First, written instructions have been employed. These are generally sent to couples before they meet their counsellors (Barker, 1984). Secondly, a number of agencies have employed a semistructured interview. In this interview, initial interviewers take a brief history of the couple's problems, partly to establish rapport and then question them on their understanding of couple counselling, expanding this knowledge with additional clearly comprehensible information relevant to the couple's particular difficulties on each of the topics outlined in the preceding paragraph on aims. The major purpose of this interview is to dispel unrealistic expectations and to induce a productive set for couple counselling on the part of the couple (Orne and Wender, 1968). Gaunt (1981) carried out a study in Birmingham comparing Relate clients who received a similar interview to that described above (known as a 'reception interview') to those whose first contact with the agency was a counselling interview. She found that those receiving a reception interview remained in counselling longer than those who did not have such an interview. However, this finding must be tempered by the fact that the time between clients' first telephone contact and first interview contact was a contaminating variable. Gaunt (1981) further interviewed 18 clients who had received a reception interview. She found that the effect of the interview was to engender a feeling of hope in clients, but that most clients did not fully understand what the interviewer said on the subject of what might happen in the counselling process. They did, however, notice quite a lot about the interviewer as a person. Gaunt also found that most interviewers had great difficulty in explaining the nature of Relate counselling to clients. It is apparent that extensive training may be necessary for interviewers to skilfully implement the tasks of the induction interview.

Thirdly, group lectures can be employed. Here a lecture is given and couples are provided with an opportunity to ask questions about the counselling process thus described. Fourthly, audio and video-tapes have been used to describe relevant details of the couple counselling process and to model productive client behaviours.

These methods vary in the amount of interaction provided between the couple and the agency representative. Most workers prefer the semistructured interview since this format provides the greatest opportunity for such interaction and allows the interviewer to tailor the information to be provided to the couple's own situation.

Work has also been done on preparing counsellors to more adequately meet clients' preferences for counselling and their therapeutic needs (Yamamoto et al., 1984). This is an important area to be considered in the UK, if clients from different cultural and socioeconomic backgrounds are going to be effectively helped with their relationship problems.

## Summary

In this chapter the concept of the therapeutic alliance was described. The point was made that a number of alliances are present in couple counselling and a number of pre-counselling influences on these alliances were discussed – couple factors, counsellor factors and agency factors. The point was made that these sets of factors interact – often in subtle and elusive ways. Finally, a number of ways of preparing couples for couple counselling were discussed. In the following chapter the emphasis will be shifted to the alliances as they unfold throughout the process of couple counselling.

## References

BARKER, R.L. (1984). *Treating Couples in Crisis*. New York: Free Press.

BORDIN, E.S. (1979). The generalizability of the psychoanalytic concept of the working alliance. *Psychotherapy: Theory, Research and Practice* 16, 252–260.

BORDIN, E.S. (1983). Myths, realities, and alternatives to clinical trials. Paper delivered at the International Conference on Psychotherapy, Bogota, Colombia.

BRANNEN, J. and COLLARD, J. (1982). *Marriages in Trouble: The process of seeking help*. London: Tavistock.

BRODERICK, C.B. (1983). *The Therapeutic Triangle: A sourcebook on marital therapy*. Beverley Hills, California: Sage.

COYNE, J.C. and WIDIGER, T.A. (1978). Toward a participatory model of psychotherapy. *Professional Psychology* 9, 700–710.

DRYDEN, W. (1985). *Therapists' Dilemmas*. London: Harper & Row.

DUCKRO, P., BEAL, D. and GEORGE, C. (1979). Research on the effects of disconfirmed client role expectations in psychotherapy: a critical review. *Psychological Bulletin* 86, 260–275.

ELLIS, A. (1983). How to deal with your most difficult client – you. *Journal of Rational–Emotive Therapy* 1, 3–8.

GARVIN, C.D. and SEABURY, B.A. (1984). *Interpersonal Practice in Social Work: Processes and procedures*. Englewood Cliffs, NJ: Prentice-Hall.

GAUNT, S. (1981). The Birmingham Marriage Guidance Council reception interview scheme. Unpublished report. Birmingham: BMGC.

GREENSON, R.R. (1967). *The Technique and Practice of Psychoanalysis*. New York: International Universities Press.

GURMAN, A.S. (1981a). Creating a therapeutic alliance in marital therapy. *American Journal of Family Therapy* 9(3), 84–87.

GURMAN, A.S. (1981b). Integrative marital therapy: toward the development of an interpersonal approach. In Budman, S.H. (Ed.) *Forms of Brief Therapy*. New York: Guilford.

HADLEY, R.G. and HADLEY, P.A. (1976). Response to task force report. *American Psychologist* **31**, 613–614.

HARPER, R.A. (1981). Limitations of marriage and family therapy. *Rational Living* **16**, 3–6.

HARTLEY, D.E. (1978). *Therapeutic alliance and the success of brief individual therapy*. Unpublished PhD dissertation, Vanderbilt University.

HARTLEY, D.E. and STRUPP, H.H. (1983). The therapeutic alliance: its relationship to outcome in brief psychotherapy. In Masling, J. (Ed.) *Empirical Studies of Psychoanalytic Theories*. Hillsdale, NJ: The Analytic Press.

HEISLER, J. (1980). The client writes. *Marriage Guidance* **19**, 115–125.

HUNT, P. (1984). Response to marriage counselling. *British Journal of Guidance and Counselling* **12**, 72–83.

HUNT, P. (1985). *Clients' responses to marriage counselling*. Unpublished PhD thesis, University of Aston in Birmingham.

IRWIN, R.S. (1980). *Client and counselor expectations of the therapeutic alliance*. Unpublished PhD dissertation, University of Michigan.

KEITHLEY, J. (1982). *Marriage counselling – general practice: an assessment of the work of marriage guidance counsellors in a general medical practice*. Unpublished PhD thesis, University of Durham.

LAZARE, A., EISENTHAL, S. and WASSERMAN, L. (1975). The customer approach to patienthood: attending to patient requests in a walk-in clinic. *Archives of General Psychiatry* **32**, 553–558.

LEHRKE, S.A. (1978). *Working alliance development early in psychotherapy*. Unpublished PhD dissertation, University of Florida.

LEVINSON, D.J., MERRIFIELD, J. and BERG, K. (1967). Becoming a patient. *Archives of General Psychiatry* **17**, 385–406.

LUBORSKY, L. (1976). Helping alliances in psychotherapy. In Claghorn, J.L. (Ed.) *Successful Psychotherapy*. New York: Brunner/Mazel.

MALUCCIO, A.N. (1979). *Learning from Clients: Interpersonal helping as viewed by clients and social workers*. New York: Free Press.

MAYER, J.E. and TIMMS, N. (1970). *The Client Speaks*. London: Routledge & Kegan Paul.

MACASKILL, N.D. and MACASKILL, A. (1983). Preparing patients for psychotherapy. *British Journal of Clinical and Social Psychiatry* **2**, 80–84.

MCDONALD, G.W. (1975). Coalition formation in marital therapy triads. *Family Therapy* **2**, 141–148.

MORAS, K. and STRUPP, H.H. (1982). Pretherapy interpersonal relations, patients' alliance, and outcome in brief therapy. *Archives of General Psychiatry* **39**, 405–409.

ORNE, M.T. and WENDER, P.H. (1968). Anticipatory socialization for psychotherapy. *American Journal of Psychiatry* **124**, 88–98.

OVERALL, B. and ARONSON, H. (1963). Expectations of psychotherapy in patients of lower socio-economic class. *American Journal of Orthopsychiatry* **33**, 421–428.

SMITH, J.W. and GRUNEBAUM, H. (1976). The therapeutic alliance in marital therapy. In Grunebaum, H. and Christ, J. (Eds) *Contemporary Marriage: Structure, dynamics and therapy*. Boston: Little, Brown & Co.

STERBA, R. (1934). The fate of the ego in analytic therapy. *International Journal of Psychoanalysis* **15**, 117–126.

WEINER, I.B. (1975). *Principles of Psychotherapy*. New York: Wiley.

YAMAMOTO, J., ASCOSTA, F.X., EVANS, L.A. and SKILBECK, W.M. (1984). Orienting therapists about patients' needs to increase patient satisfaction. *American Journal of Psychiatry* **141**, 274–277.

# Chapter 5
# Therapeutic Alliances in Couple Counselling
# II Process Issues

In this chapter, I will consider a number of issues that emerge from considering the practice of couple counselling from the vantage point of the alliances that are formed and sustained between the counsellor and the couple on the one hand and between the partners on the other. In doing so, I will raise issues and suggest solutions to particular problems from the perspective of alliance theory rather than from any one therapeutic orientation, although I recognise that such solutions are to a degree dependent upon couple counsellors' allegiances to particular orientations. The hypothesis that guides my analysis is that effective couple counselling occurs when there are strong working alliances among the participants on the three major dimensions of bonds, goals and tasks. To reiterate the point made in the previous chapter, this means that in effective couple counselling participants form and sustain sound working bonds, share a common understanding concerning the goals of the couple and agree on task-related issues (here participants (1) agree that each have tasks to accomplish in the therapeutic endeavour and agree to accomplish these tasks, and (2) understand how the execution of these tasks will lead to the attainment of the couple's therapeutic goals). Since the application of alliance theory to couple counselling is a recent development, the reader should note at the outset that the aforementioned hypothesis awaits full, empirical inquiry.

## The Processes of Negotiation and Renegotiation

The view advanced above stresses the importance of the participants reaching certain agreements on alliance-related matters. These agreements can be explicit or implicit. Whilst it is unlikely that the participants are

First published in 1985 with Patricia Hunt.

going to agree spontaneously at the outset on alliance-related matters, there has to be some way in which they can arrive at such agreements. For this to occur a process of negotiation has to be initiated at the beginning of therapy. I will focus first on how participants arrive at a shared understanding of the couple's problems, one which provides the basis for constructive change. The therapist initiates the negotiation process by striving to understand each partner's viewpoint concerning the nature of the couple's problems and what has given rise to these problems. The counsellor has to take these views seriously but also has to put forward, at some point in the process, an alternative perspective on these issues, one that not only can be used by both partners but will help them to solve their problems. In doing so, the therapist does not insist that the couple accept this view but offers it as a possible focus for the therapeutic work. In this respect, Elton (1982) has said 'it seems to me very helpful to be able to formulate the focus in such a way that the family cannot only accept it, which is essential, but also make sense of it, enlarge on it and broaden the area of work themselves' (p. 198).

As shown above, there are two major components of the negotiation process: (1) understanding and (2) persuasion (Smail, 1978). In this context persuasion means offering the couple different versions of an alternative perspective until one becomes acceptable to all concerned. The counsellor takes the couple's view into account in formulating this alternative perspective and the couple take the counsellor's views into account while making sense of their difficulties. The focus (or several foci) of the work should be the natural result of this process. In this respect, Gurman and Kniskern (1981) argue that it is important for the counsellor to offer the couple a different and unaligned view to allow them to mutually adopt a common framework and vocabulary as a starting point for change. Broderick (1983) argues that to enable a productive focus to be achieved this should incorporate the rules that appear to govern the couple system rather than emphasise the individuals' behaviours, perceptions or feelings. The negotiation process is more complex in couple counselling than it is in individual counselling, since the counsellor has not only to negotiate a shared meaning framework with each partner, but also has to help the partners achieve a workable consensus.

In this process of negotiation it is legitimate to ask which of the participants does most of the accommodating. Some interesting research by Pearlman (1977) showed that continuance in couple counselling was positively correlated with the participant's agreement on goals after four sessions of therapy (rather than at the end of the first session). Much of this goal convergence was explained by couples coming to agree with the counsellor's viewpoint rather than the counsellor radically changing his perspective. Couples who did not make this shift terminated counselling 'prematurely'.

Future study of couples' shifts in their definitions of their problems and what occasions such changes is needed. It may be that such shifts will not occur (1) if counsellors attempt to *impose* an alternative explanatory perspective on the couple, (2) if they offer implausible alternatives (that are *too* discrepant from the couple's present definitions of reality), or (3) if they refrain from offering any perspectives at all. Conversely, such shifts are likely to result when the counsellor, after communicating empathic understanding of both partners' viewpoints, offers an alternative perspective that is *moderately* discrepant from these views.

In sum, the counsellor's role in the process of negotiating about problems seems to be two-fold: (1) to communicate understanding of each person's phenomenal reality, and (2) to offer an alternative viewpoint that the couple can constructively use in the counselling work. Similar points can be made when considering how the participants negotiate constructively about therapeutic goals and tasks which will lead to the attainment of these goals.

If the counsellor succeeds in establishing a 'negotiating' set with a couple, a particular attitude has been communicated and accepted. This can be summarised thus: 'Let us see if we can arrive at a way of viewing your problems that will help you to achieve the changes you want. Furthermore, let us see if we can find mutually acceptable ways of reaching these goals.'

This 'let us see' attitude is also central to the process* of *renegotiation* which occurs when obstacles to therapeutic progress arise. Here the counsellor's view can be summarised thus: 'Let us see if we can determine what is happening to account for this situation we find ourselves in. Perhaps our focus needs to be reconsidered. Perhaps we had better look again at what we are working toward. Or could it be that we need to find different ways of achieving these goals?' Here the counsellor invites the couple to join with him or her to work out what has gone awry in the process and how it can be put right in a manner that minimises the couple's 'resistance' to therapy. When the counsellor is able to forge this kind of alliance with a couple they frequently can begin to use these principles of negotiation and renegotiation in their own life situation.

There are couples, however, for whom these processes are quite alien. For example, some couples come to couple counselling expecting to be diagnosed and treated by an 'expert'. Their attitude is: 'Tell us what to do, and we'll do it.' Numerous counsellors make the error of confronting this attitude *too* early in the therapeutic process. They may say: 'That is not how I see my role. My job is to help you decide for yourselves what to do.' Alliance theory would predict that the couple may drop out of treatment when they receive such a clear rebuttal of their therapeutic preferences. A different response in this instance might be to say something like: 'First, can you help me to understand what you have

---

*I later called this 'reflection process' – see Chapter 3.

already tried in attempting to solve your problem and why you think these haven't worked.' The counsellor can then begin to help the couple piece together a picture of what strategies have not been helpful which can in turn lead to constructive discussion about more effective alternative solutions. The counsellor in effect goes along with the couple's expectations in the first instance – 'Yes I am an expert but I need to know more about what you have tried' – and then in the process of gaining information – 'What have you tried that hasn't been helpful?' – begins to implicitly educate the couple that they can begin to work out different solutions based on their own responses to such questions. Thus the counsellor might say: 'So you both found that way unhelpful because it was too passive. What kinds of more active ways might suit you both?' The point is that sometimes a counsellor may have to accept *a portion* of a role he or she would rather not adopt in order to relinquish it more effectively later.

This raises an important dilemma in the negotiation/renegotiation process where to be directly open may lead to the dissolution of the counselling relationship. The tension here is between the 'ethical' and the 'pragmatic'. Do I, as a couple counsellor, be directly open in the negotiating process and (as shown above) risk losing this couple? Or do I adopt the 'pragmatic' approach and dodge the issue but deal with it indirectly and thus preserve the counselling relationship? Different couple counsellors will respond to this dilemma in different ways, but it is one that has to be faced. As Mattinson and Sinclair (1979) put it: 'The need to be straightforward in the initial negotiations with clients . . . is limited by the need to take into account what the client is in a position to hear' (p. 186).

When a channel of communication about alliance issues has not been established, then discrepancies between the counsellor and couple cannot be resolved. This may mean that the couple may drop out of counselling or continue in treatment but with on-going frustration (Maluccio, 1979).

# Bonds, Goals and Tasks

In this section we will consider the three components of the couple counselling alliance (see also Chapter 3).

### Bonds

It takes time to establish therapeutic bonds and the bases of such bonds between clients and counsellor may be different in different counselling relationships. Strong (1978) has noted that an initial facilitative counselling relationship may be based on *credibility* – where the client sees the counsellors as having legitimate expertise to provide help for couple problems – or on *liking* – where the client perceives the counsellor to be attractive in a way that facilitates the development of a working relationship. Couple counsellors should preferably attempt to meet the initial bonding preferences of clients which means emphasising different facets of themselves in the therapeutic interaction. This is more difficult, of course, when each partner has different preferences on this dimension.

Broderick (1983) has referred to the couple counsellor–couple relationship as the 'therapeutic triangle'. The development and maintenance of triangular rapport is one of the couple counsellors' principal tasks on the bond dimension. Perhaps the main initial component of triangular rapport concerns the degree to which partners feel deeply understood by the counsellor. Here, the task of the counsellor is to try and achieve 'empathic symmetry' in the triangle – each partner must feel equally accepted, supported and understood. The degree to which clients feel understood is significantly related to positive therapeutic outcome (see Garfield and Bergin, 1978), although this needs to be further studied in couple counselling. Some corroborating evidence, however, in couple work comes from Hunt (1985) who studied the retrospective accounts of clients concerning their responses to Relate counselling. Hunt found that the clients in her study who expressed a positive attitude towards counselling and what they gained from it made statements like 'I felt the counsellor understood me', 'There was an understanding between us', 'We got on well together and I felt that she understood and accepted me'. By contrast, clients who expressed a negative attitude about counselling referred to 'not being understood or accepted' or 'not having established a rapport with the counsellor'. Here it is not sufficient for counsellors to identify the distress of clients or even to respond to their distress but to really get into the skin of their clients and respond to the underlying issues upon which their distress is based.

In addition to 'empathic symmetry', the couple counsellor has other components to attend to in the counselling triangle so as to achieve and maintain a well-bonded relationship with the couple (Broderick, 1983). First, the counsellor should preferably develop and sustain 'spatial symmetry' between the three participants. Broderick advocates the following:

> If the arrangement of furniture in the office permits it, most therapists choose to sit in a position facing the couple and equidistant from them. If the relationship seems to be veering in one direction or the other, he or she may want to shift positions somewhat like a sailor leaning to adjust the balance in a crosswind. In our practice should we feel a husband becoming more and more distant and withdrawn as his wife recites an embarrassing inventory of his most humiliating vices, we may move physically closer to him or even touch him lightly to maintain equal contact. (p. 25)

Couples often subtly shift the position of their chairs away from each other, which makes partner–partner dialogue difficult. The counsellor should either ask them to reorient their positions to facilitate their eye contact and mutual dialogue, or comment on their increasing distance from one another. Otherwise the couple will speak to each other through the counsellor.

Secondly, counsellors should preferably try to achieve 'temporal symmetry' so that each partner has an equal opportunity to speak. To ensure that each person uses this opportunity, Broderick (1983) advocates that 'one partner should never be given the floor uninterrupted for more than a very few minutes' (p. 25). Actualising this principle helps the counsellor to show each partner that 'their interests are being served and appreciated as well as their spouse's' (Broderick, 1983, p. 26).

Preserving 'temporal symmetry' also helps the counsellor to achieve 'moral symmetry'. It is easy in couple counselling for clients to place the burden of blame for the relationship distress on the shoulders of their partner. As Broderick (1983) notes for many couples, the issue of who is the most virtuous is on the agenda from the first minutes of the first session. The counsellor has to find non-offensive means for achieving 'moral symmetry' and Broderick advocates a primary rule in this regard: 'focus on the pain each feels rather than the pain each causes' (p. 28).

In summary, the couple counsellor has to develop productive bonds with the woman as an individual, with the man as an individual and with the couple system. McDonald (1975), noting the tendency of the triads to divide into a coalition of two members against the third, advocates that 'the therapist should ideally relate to the marital unit not within the marital unit. The therapist is warned to maintain his objectivity and neutrality throughout the therapeutic process by not forming coalitions or aligning himself with either one of the marital pair' (p. 144). While I concur with this view, this should not be at the expense of the counsellor–female partner/counsellor–male partner alliances.

Threats to the development and maintenance of triangular rapport come from several sources. First, the couple's relationship with each other may preclude effective triangular counselling. Some couples are so angry toward or withdrawn from each other that their joint presence in the therapeutic setting severely threatens the other alliances. In these situations the counsellor should consider the possibility of employing counselling arenas other than conjoint couple (triangular) counselling. Secondly, the counsellor may develop countertransference reactions to one or both partners which, if unchecked, may lead to the emergence of unproductive coalitions within the triad. Thirdly, partners may develop transference feelings towards the counsellor. Hunt (1985) noted that it was the very early manifestation of negative transference reactions towards the counsellor that prevented the establishment of productive alliances in Relate counselling. Some of the clients in her study used words to describe their counsellor and his attitude in ways which were similar to how they described their partner and other people in their lives. Hunt experienced a powerful reminder of how such transference feelings even interfered with the alliance she attempted to form with her interviewees in the context of the research interview. One male client in her study reacted quite aggressively to her first question: 'How did you come to know about Marriage Guidance?' He responded as if he experienced it as a belittling question. His reply was: 'Who nowadays hasn't heard of MG? . . . I am aware of what's going on you know. I am not locked up in an attic all the time.' It emerged that this man also felt that his wife was continually criticising and denigrating him and that he had felt put down by his counsellor. As a result he had not established enough rapport with the counsellor to sustain an on-going counselling relationship.

The establishment of effective triangular bonds facilitates the later work of couple counselling but is probably neither necessary nor sufficient for a positive outcome. Writing about couple counselling, Barker (1984) has put this well: 'One of the most common mistakes therapists make . . . is to attempt an intrusive intervention without having first established rapport. On the other hand establishing rapport alone is not enough' (p. 18).

## Goals

Therapeutic goals represent what the partners wish to achieve from couple counselling. A number of issues emerge when goals are considered. First, it is more accurate to refer to a matrix of therapeutic goals. Each partner has his or her own goals for him- or herself, the partner and the relationship. Furthermore each partner has perceptions of what the other's goals are in these three areas and what preferably these goals should be. Then there are goals that represent a consensus between the partners. Finally, the counsellor's goals for each individual and the couple need to be considered and added to the matrix. Alliance theory would posit that effective couple counselling is best facilitated when the participants agree on goals chosen by *the couple* and when these goals are likely to enhance the quality of life for the couple *and* each partner.

Secondly, the couple counsellor needs to adopt an active role in helping the couple to set goals. Barker (1984, pp. 48–51) has noted that goal setting cannot be left entirely to the couple because:

1. They often are not sure of or cannot easily articulate what they want.
2. The objectives of both partners are likely to conflict.
3. Goals are usually interrelated and cannot easily be divided into desirable and undesirable parts.
4. Each partner has mixed and changing feelings about what is wanted. Thus a negotiating procedure for changing goals after counselling is underway needs to be established.
5. As noted above, the partners and the counsellor might have different views of what the goals are and should preferably be.

Thirdly, goals can be viewed along several dimensions. Goals can, for example, be placed on a specificity continuum from highly general to highly specific. Different counselling approaches are likely to help couples to set goals at different points on this continuum. Thus, behavioural couple counsellors may be more likely to help couples to set more specific goals than psychodynamically oriented couple counsellors. Goals can also be placed on an explicitness continuum. While successful couple counselling can occur without partners' goals having been made explicit, in such a circumstance counsellor and clients do have a shared implicit understanding of what the partners wish to achieve. However, the problem of keeping partners' goals at an implicit level is that these goals may be more likely to be misunderstood by both the partners and the counsellor than if they had been made explicit. Since goals change throughout the counselling process it is perhaps easier for all participants to keep a check on current goals if these have been made explicit. Some couple counsellors prefer not to make goals explicit, fearing that the counselling process may become ossified. Whilst this is a danger, it is less likely to happen when the counsellor has managed to establish and keep open the negotiation/renegotiation communication channel discussed earlier. The danger of setting goals at the outset of couple counselling is that they are more likely to be based on current states of disturbance and conflict than goals negotiated later in the process. However, the danger of not setting goals at the outset is that the couple do not know where they are heading and may become more rather than less confused. Couple counsellors need to tread carefully in this veritable minefield.

Fourthly, couple counsellors often have to deal with different types of goals. The achievement of a couple's ultimate outcome goals (i.e. what they ultimately wish to achieve as a result of counselling) may depend on them successfully reaching a set of mediating outcome goals. Couple counsellors, for example, are often faced with couples who wish to experience a more satisfying sexual relationship (ultimate outcome goal). However, it often transpires (particularly where no specific sexual dysfunction is apparent) that the couple are unable to achieve this because they are experiencing a lot of conflict in the non-sexual aspects of their relationship. In this case the counselling has to help the couple see that their outcome goal depends on the successful attainment of mediating outcome goals (i.e. improvements in the relevant non-sexual areas of their relationship). If the counsellor does not help the couple to understand these different goals and how they are linked with one another, then the alliances may be threatened because the couple may be puzzled as to why the counsellor is focusing on their non-sexual relationship when their priority is in the area of sex.

Another important distinction that needs to be made is between outcome and process goals. As employed here outcome goals refer to goals that the couple are striving to achieve *outside* the context of the counselling room whereas process goals are those that are achievable *within* the counselling room. Again the counsellor should preferably help the couple make these distinctions and see the link between process and outcome goals. Taking the above example of the couple who wish to improve their sexual relationship, the counsellor has two tasks in the realm of goals. As mentioned before, the counsellor first has to help the couple see that the achievement of their sex-related goals depend on the attainment of non-sex-related goals (e.g. they will be more likely to experience more satisfactory sex when they have learned to become more open about their differences about childrearing). Then the counsellor has to help the couple see that the achievement of this latter goal outside the counselling room depends in part upon them doing this successfully inside the room. The process–outcome distinction becomes particularly relevant for counsellors who see couples who are able to achieve their process goals but do not transfer these successes outside the immediate context of the counselling session.

Finally, distinction needs to be made between realistic and unrealistic goals. A couple may agree on a set of goals which, given the nature of their relationship, may be quite unrealistic. Rather than challenge them at the outset, the counsellor might assume the 'let us see' approach described earlier and help the couple set shorter-term objectives the attainment of which may be more realistic. It may be more helpful for the couple to discover how far they can ascend the hierarchy of their goals than for the counsellor to express doubts about these goals at the outset.

There are a number of studies that are relevant to alliance theory in the goal domain although much of this research does not focus on couple counselling. Willer and Miller (1976) found that of clients who were admitted to a psychiatric hospital those who were involved in the goal-setting process were more satisfied with and attained more from their treatment than clients who were not so involved. Client satisfaction and goal attainment were measured in this study by both clients and counsellors. Galano (1977) found that treatment at a community mental health clinic was moderately more effective when collaborative goal setting was added to goal-oriented counselling than when goals were set for clients without their collaboration. Raschella (1975) found that, in individual counselling, the greater the level of congruence which was established initially between client and counsellor in two areas – the content of treatment goals and the priority ranking of these goals – the longer these clients remained in counselling. Here, goal congruence helped to prevent premature termination of counselling. The only couple counselling study on goals was carried out by Pearlman (1977), already discussed. To reiterate, continuance in counselling was correlated with goal congruence between counsellors and couples. This only held true at the fourth session and not at the end of the initial session. As already mentioned, goal convergence was much more likely to be produced by the willingness and/or ability of the clients to alter or modify their goals than by counsellors adjusting their perception of the goals of counselling. Further research on goals in couple counselling is needed, particularly in the area where goals are related to therapeutic tasks designed to implement them.

## Tasks

Therapeutic tasks represent the means of helping couples reach their goals. All approaches to couple counselling require both the counsellor and the couple to involve themselves in the tasks that these approaches deem to be instrumental to successful couple counselling. It is the responsibility of the counsellor to implement those therapeutic strategies and techniques that are considered thus instrumental in as skilful a manner as possible. It is also the counsellor's job to help the partners to (1) acknowledge the relevance of the counsellor's tasks, (2) see how their tasks are related to the counsellor's tasks, (3) understand how implementing their tasks will help them achieve their goals, and (4) help them execute their tasks as efficiently as possible. A number of studies have been carried out on the task domain in couple or relationship-oriented counselling. In particular, these have focused on the tasks of 'talking' and exploring in the person-centred and psychodynamic counselling approaches. Maluccio (1979) found that counsellors in his study usually gave clients little explanation of the value of talk as a medium for change. Silverman (1970) in a study of dropouts from social work treatment also found that counsellors did not explain the role of talking in the counselling process and how this was related to goal achievement. She further noted that clients made a distinction between 'talking' and 'being helped'. They thus waited for the talking to end and the helping to begin and dropped out of treatment when it became apparent that 'help' would not be forthcoming. Mayer and Timms (1970) also discovered that clients found the task behaviour of their non-directive, psychodynamically oriented counsellors puzzling, and that these 'helpers' did little to provide a rationale for their own task behaviour and little to educate their clients how best to use the counselling process.

In complementary fashion, partners have to carry out therapeutic tasks if they are to reach their goals. However, two questions need to be answered in the affirmative before clients can be expected to involve themselves in the tasks of the particular approach to couple counselling that they have been offered. First, can they meet these task demands? I showed in the previous chapter that men, in general, experience greater difficulty involving themselves in the tasks of self-disclosure and self-exploration inherent in the house-style of Relate counselling than do women (Brannen and Collard, 1982; Hunt, 1985). Secondly, can clients see the relevance of carrying out these tasks? Again, men are less likely to see the relevance of the tasks of self-disclosure and self-exploration to the solutions of their problems than women (Brannen and Collard, 1982). Whether men find the execution of such tasks difficult because they fail to see their relevance or vice versa remains an open question worthy of further study.

One counselling task that needs to be considered here is 'advice' since a large minority of couples seeking couple counselling come with the expressed purpose of getting advice (Brannen and Collard, 1982; Ambrose, Harper and Pemberton, 1983). And yet most couple counsellers (certainly those working within Relate) view advice-giving as anathema to their perceived role. However, the research on the role of advice in counselling suggests that it can be an important ingredient in the change process. Reid and Shapiro (1969) distinguished among three types of advice: (1) *interrogative* – suggestions made in the form of questions (e.g. 'Have you tried calling a truce when things look as if they are getting out of control?'); (2) *declarative* – suggestions based on the professional opinion of the worker or on the research literature (e.g. 'If you want to stop physically abusing your partner, studies have shown that it is very important to significantly reduce your drinking'); and (3) *imperative* – directive statements (e.g. 'If you want your partner to be home at a certain time you should let him know your opinion and not expect him to be able to read your mind'). Ewalt and Kutz (1976) found that receptiveness to advice was positively correlated with clients' convictions that their counsellors were 'sensitive to their feelings, helped them to understand their problem, listened to them often and supported their own ideas and actions' (p. 17). Thus, far from being destructive, advice, based on strong therapeutic bonds, can be facilitative. Indeed Murphy, Cramer and Lillie (1984) found that 'talking to someone who understands' and 'advice' were the two most beneficial 'curative' factors mentioned by clients who received individual cognitive–behaviour counselling for their problems. Reid and Shapiro (1969) found that even when advice was not followed its provision stimulated clients to think about dealing with their problems in different ways and to act on these newly discovered solutions, thus dispelling the widely held belief that advice-giving inhibits clients from thinking independently. Interestingly, Ewalt and Kutz (1976) found that clients in the upper socioeconomic range preferred interrogative advice whilst those in the lower range preferred declarative advice. It is perhaps time that the role of advice in couple counselling was subjected to more objective scrutiny.

When the two partners value different task activities, this makes couple counselling a more difficult enterprise than individual counselling. In such cases it is important for the couple counsellor to address these differences. For example, when the female partner can see the relevance of verbal exploration whilst her partner prefers action-oriented methods, the counsellor may help the couple to see that both these tasks are valuable and may lead to shared goals. The male partner may be encouraged to see that action is more profitably conducted on a firm base of understanding whilst the female partner is shown that exploration needs to be translated into action. In so doing the counsellor can then ensure that both sets of expectations may be met but at different times in the process. In showing the couple that each partner's method of solving problems is legitimate and can in fact be enhanced by the utilisation of the other person's preferred style, the counsellor is indirectly helping them to achieve a greater tolerance (and hopefully greater respect) for their differences. Furthermore, they can be mutually helpful by sharing their strengths with each other.

Finally, it should be noted that both counsellors and couples have different tasks to perform at different times in the counselling process (Egan, 1982). This is especially true if the counsellor adopts an eclectic approach to marital work. At one point he or she may execute tasks designed to facilitate the couple's interpersonal dialogue whilst at another he or she may perform tasks of mediation. It probably helps strengthen the task-related alliances if the counsellor provides adequate rationales for these different tasks. The couples can also be helped to see that they have different tasks to perform at different times throughout counselling, and again the relevance of these tasks for goal achievement requires emphasis.

# Management of Therapeutic Alliances throughout the Couple Counselling Process

In this section I will consider issues that emerge from adopting a temporal perspective on the couple counselling process. Since it is likely that different alliances become salient at different times, I shall consider the development of these alliances in the initial phase of couple counselling, their maintenance in the middle phase and their dissolution in the end phase.

### The development of therapeutic alliances in the initial phase of couple counselling

Garvin and Seabury (1984) argue that when couples first approach helping agencies they have not necessarily made any commitment to work on their problems with the agency's help. Until the couple make this commitment and it is reciprocated by the counsellor and the agency, it is best to consider them as *applicants* rather than clients. As Garvin and Seabury note, at this point 'the only obligation on the part of the applicant is to explore whether or not the service is of potential use and whether he or she wishes to use it' (p. 89). Assuming that the couple's first contact is with their assigned counsellor rather than an intake worker the counsellor 'has no right to begin any process of change of the applicant or the applicant's situation until the applicant becomes a client' (Garvin and Seabury, 1984). The tasks of counsellors at this time are (1) to help the applicant come to an informed decision as to whether the service being offered is appropriate and (2) to make their own decision concerning whether or not they are the best people to help the applicant. This should of course be explained to couples at the outset. It is likely that counsellors will have different ideas concerning how detailed this negotiated process will be at this stage. Some counsellors will prefer to initiate a brief exchange of facts, a curtailed focus on problem material and a general exploration of mutual expectations, whilst others will prefer a more comprehensive and detailed pre-counselling exchange.

Once a counsellor and couple have agreed to work together a number of alliance issues become salient. In the case described above, where the couple have had an initial pre-counselling interview with their assigned counsellor, it is likely that the couple have already made preliminary judgements about their bonds with the worker. Gaunt (1981) found that while applicants for Relate counselling remembered very little about what their reception interviewer said about counselling, they remembered quite detailed personal information about their interviewers. Nonetheless, an important task of the counsellor in this initial phase of counselling is to develop and strengthen 'triangular rapport' (Broderick, 1983). The counsellor needs to join each client's own reality (Guldner, 1981) and to communicate empathic understanding of each partner's phenomenal world. Here the alliances between the counsellor and each partner receive attention. Concurrently the counsellor–couple system alliance needs attention. The counsellor needs to communicate understanding of the couple's unique problems, dysfunctional behavioural patterns and implicit agreements without siding with either partner. As Gurman (1981) has said, 'the therapist must learn to speak to both spouses at the same time' (p. 85). Finally the alliance between the partners needs early attention. Some counsellors (e.g. Barker, 1984) prefer to focus on couples' strengths or goals before considering their problems. This is to strengthen the partner–partner alliance to enable it to be sustained during problem-focused exploration.

Whilst the early alliance focus is likely to be in the bond domain there is some evidence to suggest that to neglect an early exploration of a couple's expectations in the task domain is to threaten this particular alliance. This may lead to early client drop-out or continued client frustration during the counselling process. Brannen and Collard's (1982) and Hunt's (1985) findings that men are more likely to drop out from Relate counselling because their task preferences are not being met or fully discussed is relevant here and has already been noted. Thus, if expectations (preferences and anticipations) have not been made explicit during the pre-counselling phase, they require early attention in counselling. The counsellor's task here is a complex one. He or she has to correct misconceptions and induce realistic attitudes towards and expectations for counselling, whilst instilling a sense of hope in *both* partners. Without this accompanying task of instilling hope any attempt to correct misconceptions and make explicit the nature of the help being offered may in fact have the reverse effect of enhancing despair. The counsellor needs to take care to provide a positive and credible alternative whilst correcting clients' help-seeking misconceptions. As has already been mentioned, the more the counsellor can use the couple's own data in the structuring process the more effective this process is likely to be in helping the couple to become actively involved in counselling. Finally, by promoting an open three-way exchange of views about the nature of couple counselling, the counsellor has initiated the processes of negotiation/renegotiation deemed by alliance theory to be instrumental in promoting effective counselling.

The structuring process will also be facilitated if the counsellor has some idea concerning the couple's goals. Notwithstanding the fact that goals change throughout counselling, goal-directed work helps all participants know where they are in the therapeutic process. This is particularly important for many couples in the initial phase of couple counselling, although at this stage their specified goals do not need to be too concrete.

Goals also help both the counsellor and the couple maintain a focus for their work. There is some American evidence (Noonan, 1973) to suggest that couple counselling clients expect short-term intervention and are looking for quick results. Statistics from Relate corroborate the view that couple counselling is often quite brief (90 per cent of cases are seen for between one and ten sessions – Heisler, 1984). Given the short-term nature of much couple work, it is likely that a focus helps the participants make the best use of limited time. There is indeed some evidence to show that such a focus helps to prevent early drop-out from couple counselling (Pearlman, 1977).

Alliance theory would posit that the creation of a focus should preferably be a shared one. Mayer and Timms (1970) in their research on clients' reactions to relationship-oriented social work have referred to the unreal quality of the counselling process when clients and counsellors do not have a shared focus to their work:

> There is almost a Kafkaesque quality about these worker/client interactions. To exaggerate only slightly, each of the partners assumed that the other shared certain

of his underlying conceptions about behaviour and the ways it might be altered. (p. 77)

Hunt (1985) describes the situation where counsellor and couple do not have a shared focus to their work as 'parallel tracking'. Here one or more of the participants are working on different issues and/or towards different goals than the others. To prevent the development of 'parallel tracking' an increasing number of couple counsellors advocate the use of contracts in couple work (e.g. Barker, 1984; Garvin and Seabury, 1984).

Drawing upon the work of Maluccio and Marlow (1974), a contract is defined here as: 'an explicit agreement between the therapist and the clients concerning the latter's target problems, their goals for change and the therapeutic strategies and tehniques that will be employed to help goal attainment. In addition, a working consensus will be reached concerning the roles and tasks of all participants.' It is important to note that contracts should preferably be used flexibly and are subject to revision throughout the counselling process. While some couple counsellors prefer to draw up written contracts signed by all participants, others prefer mutually agreed verbal contracts. A number of important issues relating to the use of contracts in couple counselling will now be discussed.

### Who is the contract with?

It is apparent that if only one partner in the relationship comes for counselling, the contract is with that particular partner. However, as Bennun (1984) has noted, even in this situation both counsellor and client need to consider the fact that the person is in a relationship and that the contract should reflect this. When a contract is to be made with two persons an important question which needs to be answered is this: 'Is the contract with the two individuals in the relationship or with "the relationship"?' Different workers will have different views on this point. My viewpoint is that the greater the number of alliances covered by the contract, the more effective the contract will be.

### Timing of contracts

It is important that contracts are discussed and developed when both partners are fully involved in the contract-making process. When clients are particularly distressed or preoccupied with pressing issues it would be foolhardy of the counsellor to try to involve them in the process of contract development since they may not even be able to hear what the counsellor is saying.

## Difficulties in developing contracts

Maluccio (1979) notes that, despite the fact that counsellors see the value of negotiating contracts, there remains the question as to how frequently or systematically these are employed in practice. Hunt (1985) indicated that explicit contracts between Relate counsellors and their clients were not frequently made. This was so despite the fact that the formation of explicit contracts between workers and their clients is advocated and taught during Relate counsellor training. There are a number of possible explanations for the difficulties commonly experienced by both clients and Relate counsellors when they try to develop contracts:

1. Counsellors may not have sufficient skills and experience to make a valid assessment of the couple's problems in the initial interview(s) and are therefore unable to formulate treatment goals and to make some prediction about the length of time which will be required to achieve those goals.
2. Clients may still be so preoccupied with their uncertain feelings about whether Relate is the right place for them that they are unwilling to commit themselves to counselling.
3. Many counsellors continue to operate in a person-centred manner, mainly establishing a warm relationship and facilitating the exploration of the problem, and are therefore somewhat unskilled at setting specific goals and limits. The notion that the counsellor follows 'the client' bolsters their belief that arriving at an open-ended agreement with the client is more person-centred.
4. Setting limits is often regarded as conflicting with the notion of being an all-nurturing, all-accepting, facilitating 'mother' (Temperley, 1979). Temperley comments that whilst current thinking in many fields has become free of the 'punitive, autocratic father' of the past and replaced him with the ideal of the 'nurturing, accepting, facilitating mother', education, childrearing, counselling and social work have all suffered from the idea that the 'facilitating mother' is sufficient. She says that such attitudes underestimate the inevitability of conflict and frustration and the desirability of struggle and discipline, all of which are necessary if real achievement is to occur. She suggests that there is a need to rehabilitate the limit-setting, reality-facing aspects of the 'father' in the work with clients. Counsellors commonly see their role as being a care giver and clients can seduce counsellors into this role. In such a climate, some counsellors may have difficulty in using their authority to set limits with regard to the work and to what is relevant to work on.
5. As shown in the previous chapter, clients may enter couple counselling with a variety of motivations that make the successful negotiation of effective contracts extremely difficult.

While I have focused on how to develop productive initial alliances, there is some evidence, from research on brief individual counselling, to suggest that the practitioner's initial major concern is to avoid the development of poor alliances rather than to promote the development of sound ones (Hartley and Strupp, 1983). Similarly, Bordin (1983) has noted that the strength of alliances in the initial phase of counselling does not have to be strong, but 'it must be strong enough to endure the strains of hard work in the partnership. The harder the work to be engaged in, the stronger this elementary alliance will need to be' (pp. 8–9). Further research is needed to determine the applicability of this finding to couple counselling.

## The maintenance of therapeutic alliances in the middle phase of couple counselling

Given the establishment of well-bonded alliances in the counselling triangle, the middle phase of couple counselling is characterised by a number of features. First, the task domain of the alliances is likely to come more into prominence. If an effective focus has been contractually negotiated, the counselling work is devoted primarily to the execution of tasks deemed by the participants to lead to the couple's goals. Whilst in some approaches to couple counselling the burden of change falls upon the successful execution of within-counselling tasks, other approaches place more emphasis on the couple carrying out a set of outside-counselling tasks (known as homework assignments). Once again it is important that (1) the participants understand what their tasks are, (2) they are able to execute them, and (3) they can see how the completion of these tasks can lead to the attainment of therapeutic goals. Bordin (1983) notes that the work of the partnership in the middle phase of counselling leads to strengthening of the therapeutic bonds, given that progress occurs and that the counsellor is skilful.

Secondly, the middle phase of couple counselling is characterised by modification of the couple's initial goals. This is one reason why the early establishment of the processes of negotiation/renegotiation is so important in couple counselling. If the participants are not able to talk to one another about the counselling situation, goals which have become inappropriate may not be subject to change. The changing nature of goals throughout the process of couple counselling has an effect on task-related alliances in that the employment of a variety of counselling tasks may have to be tolerated by the participants. Different counselling tasks may be best suited to effecting different therapeutic ends and couple counselling may falter if (1) the counsellor employs a restricted repertoire of tasks, (2) the partners are unwilling or unable to employ different tasks, or (3) the partners cannot tolerate the expanded task repertoire of their counsellor. Barker (1984) has underscored the fact that it is in the middle phase of counselling that the counsellor assumes different roles to help the couple achieve different goals.

Thirdly, client resistance to change can be a feature of the middle phase of couple counselling. Indeed counsellors would do well to forewarn couples that change will rarely take place in a linear fashion and that when couples do not execute tasks (either within- or outside-counselling activities), this needs to be understood by all concerned. In short, the counsellor and couple employ the 'let us see if we can understand. . .' approach outlined in the section on negotiation/renegotiation. Couple counsellors who adopt alliance theory as a way of understanding the process of couple counselling will help their clients to consider a wide range of factors whilst striving to understand the nature of the resistance. They will ask whether this resistance can be attributed to bond alliances, goal alliances and/or task alliances. Are counsellor factors mainly responsible (e.g. poor timing of intrusive interventions, failure to present a clear rationale), or client factors (e.g. one partner wishes to maintain the status quo despite overtly agreeing to pursue a particular goal)? Finally, does the reason lie somewhere in the matrix of factors within the counsellor–client interaction? Thus alliance-oriented couple counsellors will be loathe to reach the frequently heard conclusion 'this couple is not motivated' without having undertaken with the couple an extensive investigation into the nature of the resistance.

If couple counsellors are sensitive to alliance-related issues, they are unlikely to become bogged down with a couple in an interminable counselling relationship which seems to be without direction and purpose. Also such counsellors are less likely to have clients who remain in counselling but do so with frustration. Maluccio (1979) found that clients in a type of counselling (relationship oriented social work) not characterised by negotiation between counsellors and clients either dropped out early in treatment or continued disillusioned and frustrated. This pattern was not found in counselling relationships where on-going negotiation and renegotiation was a major feature of the interaction.

Whilst a lot more work on the maintenance of therapeutic alliances needs to be done in the middle phases of couple counselling, some interesting suggestions come from the work of Bordin (1983). Writing primarily about individual counselling, Bordin's view is that the strength of the alliance increases in the middle phase of counselling given the skill of the counsellor, and that the repair of momentary breaks in the alliances can of itself be extremely facilitative. In couple counselling, however, there are several alliances and thus the strength of each individual alliance may not develop to the capacity as it does in individual work. Nevertheless, Bordin's view has an interesting parallel in couple work. It may be that the strength of the alliance *between* partners is enhanced when *they* succeed in repairing the 'breaks' in their relationship. The more they succeed in doing so using their own resources, the stronger their alliance with one another will become. Conversely, the more the counsellor assumes major responsibility for this 'repair' work, the weaker the partners' joint alliance will be; hence the preference, echoed by couple counsellors of all persuasions, for couples to do most of their own work. Yet the skill of the counsellor is to enable them to do so.

### The dissolution of therapeutic alliances in the end phase of couple counselling

One of the prime tasks of the couple counsellor in the middle phase of treatment, then, is to help the couple strengthen their own working alliance. If the work goes well and progress begins to be maintained, the task of the counsellor is to dissolve the alliances between him- or herself and the couple system without weakening the partner–partner alliance. It is not sufficient for the counsellor just to help the couple achieve their goals and then withdraw, but rather he or she needs to help the couple become their own change agents. The ultimate goal of couple counselling, when the partners decide to remain together, is to help the couple utilise and internalise methods for solving future problems and to discourage the couple from returning for help as soon as problems materialise in their relationship. Thus, when couple counselling has gone well, the counsellor's goal is to encourage the couple to view themselves as their own therapeutic change agents. This can best be done by reviewing the course of counselling with the couple, emphasising the methods that the couple have employed to overcome their problems, and discussing how these methods might be employed in the future.

When the course of couple counselling has run smoothly, termination of the triangular relationship tends to occur as a natural culminating stage of all that has gone before. In such cases, the couple may find it difficult to bring up issues for discussion or the session tends to be characterised by social as opposed to therapeutic discourse. There are different ways of dissolving the triangular alliances. Some counsellors prefer to increase the length of time between sessions (i.e. gradual disengagement), whilst others prefer to set the date of the final session at the outset of the end phase. According to alliance theory, counsellors should preferably be guided by the unique wishes of the couple when deciding upon a mode of dissolving triangular alliances. What is important, however, is that termination should best be employed as a way of stabilising counselling outcome (and hopefully enhancing future growth). This dictates that the couple's goals should have been attained fairly well in advance of the final session (Barker, 1984).

In successful cases of couple counselling, dissolution of the triangular alliances is less difficult than disengagement in individual counselling. 'The

one-to-one relationship between therapist and individual client accentu-
ates an intense interpersonal connectedness, mutual empathy, transference
and countertransference, and strong reluctance to give it up' (Barker,
1984, p. 97); whereas, when couple counselling has produced a positive
outcome, the intensity of this 'interpersonal connectedness' is greatest
between the partners themselves. Yet, despite the fact that the couple
counsellor seeks to adopt a lower profile in the latter stages of the work,
there is bound to be some ambivalence on the part of the couple in
disengaging from someone who has been helpful. It is constructive if all
parties can acknowledge the mixed feelings of positive optimism and
sadness that usually accompany a healthy life transition with all its gains
and losses.

However, the dissolution of triangular alliances can frequently be fraught
with problems. Obviously couple counselling can be terminated prematurely, i.e. before the couple has achieved and stabilized their goals, and
this is frequently a sign that triangular alliances have not been adequately
formed or are not strong enough to sustain the participants through the
task demands of the counselling. In this regard, Broderick (1983) has
argued that 'when the triangular relationship aborts early it is because the
therapist was not able to establish symmetrical rapport with the couple'
(p. 159).

Maluccio (1979) prefers to distinguish between planned and unplanned
termination rather than refer to premature termination. He found that in
some cases when termination was unplanned the clients felt they had
achieved their goals but their counsellors felt that there was still more
work to be done – hence unplanned termination. In these cases 'the clients
were satisfied with having obtained help in relation to specific "problems
in living", while workers were concerned with overall "cures" or broad
changes in an individual's situation or personality structure' (p. 182). The
counsellors of these satisfied clients seemed to disregard the importance
of clients' goals and overestimated the importance of the therapeutic
bonds as catalysts for change. Their clients, however, reported that
counselling had had a triggering effect in that it helped them to utilise
better the external resources in their community, i.e. it enabled clients to
form more productive alliances with outside helping agents.

Maluccio's second group of unplanned terminators were indeed
dissatisfied with the service offered and there were clear *early* signs of
unformed or weakly formed therapeutic alliances.

> Clients and workers in these cases had a vague sense of what could be happening in
> treatment, were unable to establish an emotional connection between them, did not
> actively engage in contract negotiation, and ended the first session with marked
> vagueness and uncertainty about future plans. (Maluccio, 1979, p. 181)

In Hunt's (1985) study of clients' reactions to Relate counselling over
half of her client sample ended counselling by default either by cancelling

or failing to attend appointments. She concluded that negotiation of therapeutic contracts may have minimised the incidence of unplanned endings. Furthermore, Hunt found in interviewing this group that many were left with unresolved feelings about their counselling experience and tried, in her view, to use the research interview as a way of reaching a more satisfactory conclusion to their contact with Relate.

Hunt also found that unplanned termination was due in part to the failure of the participants to renegotiate a different kind of contract, particularly when couples decided to separate or divorce. This may be due to (1) clients' perception of Relate as a 'marriage mending' agency and therefore not an appropriate service for dealing with 'marriage ending' matters, or to (2) counsellors' difficulties in renegotiating counselling contracts. Further research is indicated here.

Major problems can occur when termination is avoided as an issue. Sometimes couple counsellors and couples get hopelessly bogged down in counselling, when it might be better to terminate the particular counselling relationship with a possible referral to a more appropriate helper. Counselling relationships get bogged down for many reasons but one identifying characteristic of such partnerships is failure to establish and maintain the negotiation/renegotiation process. As a result there develops a kind of collusive norm between the participants which inhibits the discussion of meta-counselling issues (i.e. issues about the counselling). Supervision could be instrumental in helping the couple counsellor to understand the relevant factors here (often pertaining to the counsellor–couple interaction or to the existence of partner 'secrets') and thence to intervene differently – if indeed the worker is prepared to bring the case to supervision!

Broderick (1983) has noted that overdependency is another characteristic of counselling where the issue of termination is avoided.

> On the couple's side they may come to view the therapist as a powerful stabilizing influence on the runaway destructiveness of their relationship. Like the one-eyed man in the land of the blind the therapist may become, not king, but captive – too valuable to be allowed to escape. (p. 166)

This couple dynamic can complement the counsellor's *need* to be helpful and/or needed and the counselling relationship continues until one or both parties challenge their neurotic needs.

The counsellor's contribution to 'interminable' couple work often centres on two issues as noted by Broderick (1983):

> ... the therapist may fall into the role of warm, supportive parent to a couple who never had one in either of their growing-up experience... or the therapist may become seduced into an enmeshed relationship because of his own unfinished business with his own parents or siblings or children. (pp. 166–167)

Overdependency in the bond alliances thus interferes with the establishment of 'mature' bonds where the counsellor is a temporary member of the triangle striving to help the couple to ally themselves with each other. Under these conditions the task of dissolving the therapeutic alliances cannot be successfully attempted.

Finally, many couple counsellors offer couples follow-up session(s) to monitor the stability of change. Barker (1984) urges counsellors 'to individualize the follow-up to suit the unique needs and circumstances of each couple who successfully terminate treatment' (p. 99). Research on the impact of follow-up sessions on triangular alliances would be fruitful in that the status of such sessions is somewhat ambiguous. They are not a part of the counselling and yet they are experiences shared by the members of the dissolved counselling relationship.

# Summary

In this chapter, the focus was on the therapeutic alliances as they develop throughout couple counselling. Negotiation and renegotiation processes have to be initiated and sustained throughout the work if alliance issues are to be openly and constructively discussed by counsellors and couples. These issues centre on the bonds that develop in the triangular relationship, the goals of the couple and the tasks which are executed by all participants in the service of these goals. Finally, a temporal analysis of couple counselling alliances was presented as these occur in the initial, middle and end phases of this type of work.

# References

AMBROSE, P., HARPER, J. and PEMBERTON, R. (1983). *Surviving Divorce: Men beyond marriage*. Brighton: Wheatsheaf Books.

BARKER, R.L. (1984). *Treating Couples in Crisis*. New York: Free Press.

BENNUN, I. (1984). Evaluating marital therapy: a hospital and community study. *British Journal of Guidance and Counselling* 12(1), 84–91.

BORDIN, E.S. (1983). Myths, realities, and alternatives to clinical trials. Paper delivered at the International Conference on Psychotherapy, Bogota, Colombia.

BRANNEN, J. and COLLARD, J. (1982). *Marriages in Trouble: The process of seeking help*. London: Tavistock.

BRODERICK, C.B. (1983). *The Therapeutic Triangle: A sourcebook on marital therapy*. Beverley Hills, CA: Sage.

EGAN, G. (1982). *The Skilled Helper: Model, skills, and methods for effective helping*, 2nd edn. Monterey, California: Brooks/Cole.

ELTON, A. (1982). Maintaining family motivation during treatment. In Bentovim, A., Gorell Barnes, G. and Cooklin, A. (Eds) *Family Therapy: Complementary frameworks of theory and practice*. Volume 1. London: Academic Press.

EWALT, P.L. and KUTZ, J. (1976). An examination of advice giving as a therapeutic intervention. *Smith College Studies in Social Work* 47, 3–19.

GALANO, J. (1977). *Increased treatment effectiveness as a function of increased client involvement in therapy.* Unpublished PhD dissertation, Bowling Green State University.

GARFIELD, S.L. and BERGIN, A.E. (Eds) (1978). *Handbook of Psychotherapy and Behavior Change*, 2nd edn. New York: Wiley.

GARVIN, C.D. and SEABURY, B.A. (1984). *Interpersonal Practice in Social Work: Processes and procedures.* Englewood Cliffs, NJ: Prentice-Hall.

GAUNT, S. (1981). The Birmingham Marriage Guidance Council reception interview scheme. Unpublished report, Birmingham: BMGC.

GULDNER, C.A. (1981). Premature termination in marital and family therapy. In Gurman, A.S. (Ed.) *Questions and Answers in the Practice of Family Therapy.* New York: Brunner/Mazel.

GURMAN, A.S. (1981). Creating a therapeutic alliance in marital therapy. *American Journal of Family Therapy* **9**(3), 84–87.

GURMAN, A.S. and KNISKERN, D.P. (1981). Family therapy outcome research: knowns and unknowns. In Gurman, A.S. and Kniskern, D.P. (Eds) *Handbook of Family Therapy.* New York: Brunner/Mazel.

HARTLEY, D.E. and STRUPP, H.H. (1983). The therapeutic alliance: its relationship to outcome in brief psychotherapy. In Masling, J. (Ed.) *Empirical Studies of Psychoanalytic Theories.* Hillsdale, NJ: The Analytic Press.

HEISLER, J. (1984). *The National Marriage Guidance Council Client 1982.* Rugby: NMGC.

HUNT, P. (1985). *Clients' responses to marriage counselling.* Unpublished PhD thesis, University of Aston in Birmingham.

MALUCCIO, A.N. (1979). *Learning from Clients: Interpersonal helping as viewed by clients and social workers.* New York: Free Press.

MALUCCIO, A.N. and MARLOW, W.D. (1974). The case for the contract. *Social Work* **19**, 28–36.

MATTINSON, J. and SINCLAIR, I. (1979). *Mate and Stalemate: Working with marital problems in a social services department.* Oxford: Blackwell.

MAYER, J.E. and TIMMS, N. (1970). *The Client Speaks.* London: Routledge & Kegan Paul.

MCDONALD, G.W. (1975). Coalition formation in marital therapy triads. *Family Therapy* **2**, 141–148.

MURPHY, P.M., CRAMER, D. and LILLIE, F.J. (1984). The relationship between curative factors perceived by patients in their psychotherapy and treatment outcome: an exploratory study. *British Journal of Medical Psychology* **57**, 187–192.

NOONAN, J.R. (1973). A follow-up of pretherapy dropouts. *Journal of Community Psychology* **1**, 43–45.

PEARLMAN, S. (1977). *Convergence of therapist and client goals in the initial stage of marital counselling and its relationship to continuance in treatment.* Unpublished PhD dissertation, University of Toronto.

RASCHELLA, G.F. (1975). *An evaluation of the effect of goal congruence between client and therapist on premature client dropout from therapy.* Unpublished PhD dissertation, University of Pittsburgh.

REID, W.J. and SHAPIRO, B.L. (1969). Client reactions to advice. *Social Science Review* **43**, 165–173.

SILVERMAN, P.R. (1970). A re-examination of the intake procedure. *Social Casework* **51**, 625–634.

SMAIL, D.J. (1978). *Psychotherapy: A personal approach.* London: Dent.

STRONG, S.R. (1978). Social psychological approach to psychotherapy research. In Garfield, S.L. and Bergin, A.E. (Eds) *Handbook of Psychotherapy and Behavior Change*, 2nd edn. New York: Wiley.

TEMPERLEY, J. (1979). The implications for social work practice of recent psychoanalytical developments. Paper presented at a conference on 'Change and renewal in psychodynamic social work', Oxford.

WILLER, B. and MILLER, G.H. (1976). Client involvement in goal setting and its relationship to therapeutic outcome. *Journal of Clinical Psychology* **32**, 687–690.

# Chapter 6
# Eclectic Approaches in Individual Counselling: Some Pertinent Issues

A consideration of dictionary definitions of 'eclecticism' would yield a common theme – that of selecting from diverse systems. Whilst some definitions emphasise the selection of what is best from these diverse sources, others make no such judgement. Whilst some definitions include the activity of attempting to combine harmoniously the selections, others are silent in this respect. This situation is parallelled when the views of practitioners who deem themselves to be 'eclectics' are considered (Lazarus, 1976; Brammer and Shostrom, 1977; Garfield and Kurtz, 1977). It becomes readily apparent that to refer to *the* 'eclectic' approach to counselling falls prey to a 'uniformity myth' (Kiesler, 1966) and that such a reference is to be avoided. Rather there is a need to consider what 'eclectics' actually do as well as what they say they do (Garfield and Kurtz, 1977) and consequently to try and tease out the effective ingredients common to 'eclectic' approaches. Presently, we are a long way from such a position. However, by clarifying some of the issues pertinent to the study of 'eclectic' approaches to individual counselling, it is hoped to move a little closer to this goal.

## Eclectic Approaches vs Single Theoretical Approaches

Although there are some advantages in adhering to a single theoretical approach to counselling – namely (1) counsellors have a ready-made system of assumptions and concepts and thus are encouraged to feel secure; (2) an extensive experience and database is provided; and (3) consistency of method and theory is found (Brammer and Shostrom, 1977) – Garfield and Kurtz (1977) found increasing dissatisfaction with the single

---

First published in 1980.

theoretical approach to counselling. In their survey of 154 American clinical psychologists, who had designated themselves as 'eclectics', a common theme expressed was that 'no current theory was adequate for handling the diversity of clients seen in practice and that clinicians must select the approach that best fits a given client' (Garfield and Kurtz, 1977, p. 78).

In addition to a restricted view of data, adhering to a single theoretical viewpoint encourages dogmatism and distortion. As Wachtel (1977) notes when writing about the psychodynamic and behavioural frameworks.

> It is my experience that workers guided by either of these two broad frames of reference tend to have only a rather superficial knowledge (and sometimes none at all) of the important regularities observed by those guided by the other viewpoint. Each defends his or her own position by caricaturing the other and by so doing avoids any basic change in viewpoint. (pp. 5–6)

Whilst eclectic viewpoints are increasing in popularity, it may well be that some counsellors may do better with clients by retaining allegiance to a single theoretical approach since their attempts at integration may lead to methods being used haphazardly, shotgun fashion. These counsellors may wander around in a daze of professional nihilism experimenting with new 'fad' methods indiscriminately (Thorne, 1973). Indeed this latter group would lead themselves into a therapeutic world inhabited by:

> . . . a mish-mash of theories, a huggermugger of procedures, a gallimaufry of therapies and a charivaria of activities having no proper rationale and incapable of being tested or evaluated. (Eysenck, 1970, p. 145)

Whilst 'eclectic' approaches do not have to lead us into such a nightmarish world, a lot more needs to be known about what Lazarus, Shostrom and others actually do that lead them into greener pastures.

Lazarus (1976) notes how his therapeutic effectiveness increased, in that his clients showed greater durable change, when he broadened his therapeutic approach to cover more modalities of human functioning. We can speculate, however, that adopting an 'eclectic' stance might yield 'for better or worse' results with regard to clinical effectiveness.

# The Role of Theory in the 'Eclectic' Approaches

In their struggle towards integration* different counsellors emphasise different aspects of the enterprise. Lazarus (1967), for example, urges his fellow counsellors to equip themselves with a wide range of effective techniques culled from a wide range of theoretical systems. He stresses that there is no need to accept the originator's theoretical reason for the

---

*It is now believed that eclecticism and integration are different activities. The reader is referred to Dryden and Norcross (1990) for a detailed discussion of this point.

effectiveness of a given technique. Subsequently Lazarus was attacked for being atheoretical, although recently he has placed his therapeutic endeavours under the umbrella of social learning theory (Lazarus, 1976).

Whereas theory is de-emphasised by Lazarus it is stressed by Brammer and Shostrom (1977) who contrast their own 'creative synthesis' approach with the pragmatism of 'eclectics' such as Lazarus. In creative synthesis the focus is on the development of an ever-changing and extending *personal* system and integrative theorising at the personal level is encouraged.

Whilst Lazarus (1967, 1976) has argued that counsellors do not have to concern themselves unduly with complex theoretical integration while using methods derived from diverse sources, elsewhere he states:

> The individual practitioner's view of disturbing behaviour is apt to determine the methods of treatment he applies or withholds in every case. (Lazarus, 1974, p. 98)

Whereas the theories which counsellors have in their heads with regard to the acquisition and maintenance of human dysfunctioning will, in a broad sense, influence their therapeutic methods, how specific will this influence be? Sundland (1977) has shown that when we come to try and understand counsellors' moment-to-moment therapeutic behaviour, knowing their personal theories of human dysfunctioning may not account for a large proportion of the variance.

That the broad integration of therapeutic methods derived from disparate theoretical viewpoints is possible has been shown by Wachtel (1977). Wachtel, a psychoanalytically trained counsellor, was helped to integrate broadly behavioural and psychodynamic methods by his own shift in theoretical perspective. Drawing upon Sullivan's interpersonal theory, Wachtel argues that disturbed behaviour is maintained not by a constellation of psychic forces established in childhood (and 'frozen' in the unconscious) but by the way the person presently lives his or her life. His or her present behaviour produces a reaction in others which in turn helps to maintain pathological structures of perception, thought and feeling. The client can be helped to 'break' such vicious circles by *both* the counsellor's analytical inquiry *and* the utilisation of behavioural methods. Here is an example of a counsellor who is able to both assimilate and accommodate new input.

Such sensitive use of assimilation and accommodation processes is helpful if the counsellor is to avoid using incompatible procedures. As an illustration let us consider the counsellor who adheres to the rational–emotive viewpoint that self-esteem, i.e. the person rating his or her totality, is pernicious and that instead the client would do well to accept rather than rate him- or herself. For our counsellor, then, any procedure which encourages the client to rate rather than accept him- or herself is to be avoided. In this respect the clinician had better consider both the short-term and long-term implications of therapeutic procedures. A procedure may help the client feel less depressed in the short term but encourage him or her to continue rating him- or herself in the long term (see Chapter 9).

How broadly must 'eclectic' counsellors conceptualise disturbed behaviour? According to Lazarus they must have a very broad way of conceptualising human dysfunction. His own way of achieving this broadly based view is to consider dysfunctioning across seven basic modalities (behavioural, affective, sensory, imaginal, cognitive, interpersonal and drug). Presumably the acquisition and perpetuation of such dysfunctioning can be explained by social learning theory – Lazarus's theoretical umbrella.

## The Counsellor's Decision-making Processes in the Eclectic Approaches

It is my contention that eclectic counsellors are guided by some cognitive map to enable them to choose among the many therapeutic options open to them. It is such knowledge as this that would help illuminate our search for effective ingredients in the 'eclectic' approaches. In this regard Meichenbaum (1977) has argued for the study of what counsellors say to themselves when faced with the problems of (1) making sense of what their clients tell them and (2) selecting therapeutic techniques. Dimond and Havens (1975) have argued that faced with such a choice the counsellor 'obviously ... would be determined by a decision as to which theory most closely approximates his patient's phenomenology ...' (p. 198). The danger here lies in the application of methods derived from a particular theoretical viewpoint so that a clinician may be person-centred with one patient, a Freudian with another and so on. Such a position as well as discouraging theoretical integration would place quite a strain on the personal resources of the counsellor!

A more enlightened approach would be for the counsellor to consider initially his or her therapeutic strategy. Then, depending on a range of client variables which would include degree of expected resistance, client readiness (timing being crucial) and the client's personal resources, the counsellor would then choose the technique which he or she considered best suited to implementing the strategy. It is clear that the counsellor had better have a broad range of skills and methods at his or her fingertips if he or she is to be successful. This strategy-oriented approach has been advocated by Goldfried (1978) who argues that our search for therapeutic commonalities among systems is best directed at the level of intervention strategies 'which exist at a level of abstraction somewhere between theory and technique' (p. 29). Goldfried (1978) considers that:

> If we can indeed ever reach the point where we agree on some common intervention strategies the next step would be a more empirical one. This would entail the specification of various techniques for implementing each strategy and a comparison

of the relative effectiveness of each of these techniques together with their interaction with problems and individual differences among clients. (p. 29)

This, of course, is the oft-heard cry for greater specificity in counselling research. But would our competent 'eclectic' be able to use such useful information, dispassionately. I would venture not since he or she will also be a fallible human being (Ellis and Harper, 1975), prone to the effects of countertransference. Thus faced with a client who is talking about how 'all women are the same − smothering', our 'eclectic' counsellor may be threatened by such a statement and choose a more distancing technique than might be advisable. Also counsellors feel more comfortable using some techniques than others and this would probably be a factor in technique selection. In this respect Shoeninger (1965) found that clients were able to detect whether or not a counsellor was comfortable disclosing information about him- or herself. The counsellor who was more comfortable in the self-disclosure condition than in the non-self-disclosure condition was perceived by clients as more genuine, positively regarded and empathic in the self-disclosure condition. However, the two counsellors who were more comfortable in the non-self-disclosure condition received significantly higher ratings on the dependent variables in that condition than they did in the self-disclosure condition.

It is crucial for 'eclectic' counsellors to monitor the effects that their technical procedures have on their clients. This can be done in a number of ways, including directly asking the client how he or she experienced the procedure, and observing the effect of the procedure on client verbal and non-verbal behaviour in the interview. This may also provide a useful guide for the counsellor with respect to the possible effectiveness of future interventions. More broadly, the 'eclectic' counsellor had better be aware that each of the different stances that he or she may take with clients may have anti-therapeutic consequences for some. Silverman (1974) has written that different stances have different 'transference pulls'. For example, a directive stance may encourage certain clients to view the counsellor as authoritarian which may interfere with treatment. An 'eclectic' stance (since it makes more variability than single-approach stances) may not be therapeutic for clients who have received inconsistent treatment from significant others. Recent theorists (Goldberg, 1977; Smail, 1978) consider counselling to be a process of negotiation between counsellor and client. Thus, it may be that 'eclectic' counsellors may profit from explaining to clients, in advance, the purpose behind their planned interventions and to negotiate their use with the client. Such a procedure may, in addition, minimise the 'transference pull' of the stances which 'eclectic' counsellors may adopt during counselling.

The study of counsellors' decision-making processes at impasses would be another instructive area for study. Whenever he reaches an impasse

Lazarus asks himself whether he has neglected working within a particular modality with a client. He has found that focusing on the neglected modality often yields therapeutic gain. The 'eclectic' counsellor has a much broader range of variables to consider when an impasse has been reached and thus we might predict that his or her 'self-talk' would be more varied than the single-school practitioner. A Wolpean, for example, faced with an impasse might ask himself whether he had relaxed his client sufficiently deeply, whether the steps between hierarchy items were too large, and so on.

In addition to learning about the decision-making processes of skilled 'eclectic' counsellors we also need to have 'more *explicit* criteria concerning the choice of different techniques coupled with less reliance upon subjective judgment' (Lazarus, 1976).

It is the present thesis that together, the empirical and the phenomenological approach to the study of the way 'eclectics' work will shed more light on these activities than will each approach employed separately. I quote a lengthy statement by Lazarus (1978) because it places this issue in sharp focus:

> ... Science's contribution to therapy comes in rather broad units that formulate general connection between antecedents and consequences, but that science has offered very little guidance through moment-to-moment decision-making processes. To cite an obvious example, when I select systematic desensitization as one of the techniques to be used with a given client, I do so because scientific studies have suggested that this method has a high success rate in certain instances. (p. 24)

This is the strength of the empirical approach giving the client information concerning the conditions under which a particular technique might be appropriate. Lazarus (1978) continues:

> But the different ways in which I explain its rationale to specific clients, the individual pace, manner and structure I employ with different people and the variety of ways in which I introduce scenes embroider images, and embellish tailor-made themes, rests heavily on 'intuition', 'clinical experience' and on 'educated guesses', these variables have little to do with science. In my view, it is artistic skill rather than scientific acumen that separates creative therapists from mediocre technicians. (p. 24)

The challenge is there for researchers to develop a methodology appropriate to the study of clinical intuition. It is my contention that such an enterprise is best carried out in the spirit of phenomenology with researchers helping creative counsellors to make explicit the automatic processes which underpin the process of intuition.

# References

BRAMMER, L.M. and SHOSTROM, E.L. (1977). *Therapeutic Psychology: Fundamentals of counseling and psychotherapy*, 3rd edn. Englewood Cliffs, NJ: Prentice-Hall.

DIMOND, R.E. and HAVENS, R.A. (1975). Restructuring psychotherapy: toward a prescriptive eclecticism. *Professional Psychology* May, 193–200.

DRYDEN, N. and NORCROSS, J.C. (Eds) (1990). *Electicism and Integration in Counselling and Pyschotherapy.* London: Gale Centre.

ELLIS, A. and HARPER, R.A. (1975). *A New Guide to Rational Living.* Englewood Cliffs, NJ: Prentice-Hall.

EYSENCK, H.J. (1970). A mish-mash of theories. *International Journal of Psychiatry* 9, 140–146.

GARFIELD, S.L. and KURTZ, R. (1977) A study of eclectic views. *Journal of Consulting and Clinical Psychology* 45, 78–83.

GOLDBERG, C. (1977). *Therapeutic Partnership: Ethical concerns in psychotherapy.* New York: Springer.

GOLDFRIED, M.R. (1978). On the search for effective intervention strategies. *The Counseling Psychologist* 7(3), 28–30.

KIESLER, D.J. (1966). Some myths of psychotherapy research and the search for a paradigm. *Psychological Bulletin* 65, 110–136.

LAZARUS, A.A. (1967). In support of technical eclecticism. *Psychological Reports* 21, 415–416.

LAZARUS, A.A. (1967). Desensitization and cognitive restructuring. *Psychotherapy: Theory, Research and Practice* 11(2), 98–102.

LAZARUS, A.A. (1976). *MultiModal Behavior Therapy.* New York: Springer.

LAZARUS, A.A. (1978). Science and beyond. *The Counseling Psychologist* 7(3), 24–25.

MEICHENBAUM, D.H. (1977) *Cognitive Behaviour Modification.* New York: Plenum.

SCHOENINGER, D.W. (1965). *Client experiencing as a function of therapist self-disclosure and pre-therapy training in experiencing.* Unpublished Doctoral Dissertation, University of Wisconsin. (Abstract in *Dissertation Abstracts International*, 1966 26(9), 5551.)

SILVERMAN, L.H. (1974). Some psychoanalytic considerations of non-psychoanalytic therapies: on the possibility of integrating treatment approaches and related issues. *Psychotherapy: Theory, Research and Practice* 11(4), 298–305.

SMAIL, D.J. (1978). *Psychotherapy: A personal approach.* London: Dent.

SUNDLAND, D.M. (1977). Theoretical orientations of psychotherapists. In Gurman, A.S. and Razin, A.M. (Eds) *Effective Psychotherapy: A Handbook of Research.* Oxford: Pergamon Press.

THORNE, F.C. (1973) An eclectic evaluation of psychotherapeutic methods. In Jurjevich, R.R. (Ed.) *Direct Psychotherapy: 28 American Originals*, Volume 2. Coral Gables, Florida: University of Miami Press.

WACHTEL, P.L. (1977). *Psychoanalysis and Behavior Therapy.* New York: Basic Books.

# Chapter 7
# A Model of Counsellor Decision-making in Individual Eclectic Counselling

As noted in the previous chapter eclecticism has been defined as selecting what appears to be best from diverse therapeutic sources, systems and styles. In order to explain this process of selection, a model of counsellor decision-making will be put forward in this chapter (Figure 7.1). This model can be used as an aid to understanding the decisions that counsellors make in the process of counselling whether or not they adopt an eclectic stance. It is my contention that studying counsellor decision-making in eclectic counselling is probably the best way of understanding what eclectic counsellors actually do in practice.

In summary, the model shows that, despite some arguments to the contrary, eclectic counsellors are more or less guided by theoretical concepts which are, in turn, determined in part by a set of personal factors. The theoretical notions which underpin the work of eclectic counsellors determine in the first instance a set of counselling strategies that in turn determine what range of techniques or methods is selected for possible use with a particular client. Counselling techniques are made up of a number of counsellor–client response exchanges.

The major elements in the model and the factors that influence them will be specified in greater detail below. However, it is worth while noting at this juncture that eclectic counsellors, like other counsellors, are influenced by a set of imprecise personal factors which guide their behaviour. A number of writers have written on the topic of therapist intuition. Although it is my contention that studies which focus on counsellor decision-making in counselling are probably the best route to understand this intuitive process, it must be recognised, however, that we may never be able to *fully* understand what guides therapists in their selection of strategies, techniques and specific responses. A good example of this appears in the work of Standal and Corsini (1959). In this edited

First published in 1984.

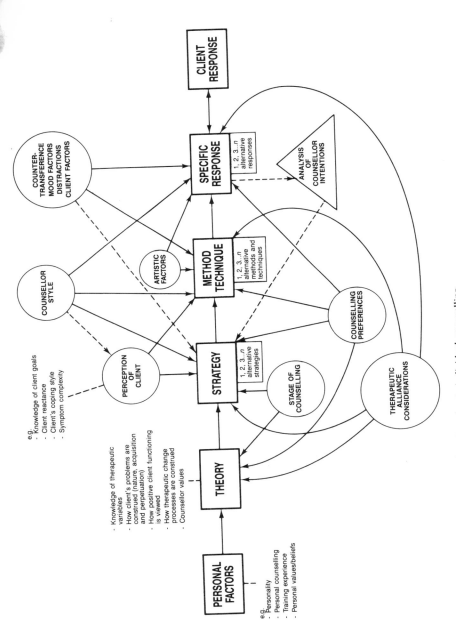

**Figure 7.1**  A model of counsellor decision-making in eclectic individual counselling

book a number of counsellors outlined how they handled 'critical' incidents in counselling. The conclusion which can be gained from this material is that counsellors often handle such critical incidents in a 'spontaneous' fashion which they do not fully understand either at the time or even after some reflection. Indeed, their attempts to make sense of these experiences after the event are open to the accusation of post-hoc rationalisation. With this in mind the model of counsellor decision-making will now be presented.

# The Role of Theory in Counsellor Decision-making

Cornsweet (1983) has argued that a theory in counselling is 'primarily a model, a way of structuring and understanding a complex set of phenomena. It provides the clinician, in particular, with a framework from which to view the patient and with a rationale for intervention' (p. 308). In this sense, counsellors cannot help but be theoretical in that (1) they structure what they observe, and (2) this structuring is based on explicit or implicit assumptions which influence their actions to some degree. Thus counsellors who claim to be atheoretical and conduct counselling in a highly individualistic, eclectic fashion are in fact probably operating from an implicit, informal system of beliefs; whilst counsellors who choose not to understand why client problems develop or why therapeutic techniques work and merely use those techniques that are deemed to be effective are, as Cornsweet (1983) has shown, operating from a 'radical empirical theory which operates on observational data alone' (p. 311).

A current view of counselling effectiveness is that outcome is dependent on a process of persuasion or social influence. 'Successful' clients, according to this view, emerge from counselling more closely identified with the beliefs of their counsellors (Beutler, 1983). It is therefore important for counsellors to be reasonably consistent in their beliefs or values if they are not to 'persuade' clients to adopt a set of incoherent, contradictory beliefs. This suggests that eclectic counsellors should pay close attention to their implicit assumptions and think through important theoretical issues. Important issues, in my opinion, include: (1) the image of the person; (2) how psychological disturbance and health are construed; (3) how psychological problems develop and are perpetuated; and (4) how therapeutic change processes are construed. It is, however, debatable whether all these factors have equal influence in determining which strategies eclectic counsellors develop in treatment. Davis (1983), for example, has argued that the way counsellors understand the *origin* of a problem may have little influence in determining which counselling procedures are selected for dealing with the problem. In addition, a knowledge of therapeutic variables (common factors) will enhance eclectic counsellors' theory of counselling (Garfield, 1980).

It is understandable that some eclectic counsellors shy away from an examination of their theoretical assumptions, since at first sight it seems as if to attempt a theoretical integration of several established perspectives is an insurmountable task. However, as Davis (1983) has shown, monolithic theories do not need to be swallowed whole and theories constantly evolve. Eclectics do not need to integrate all parts of all available theories, but only those parts which have validity and are helpful clinically. Wachtel (1977) has shown that such meaningful integration is possible and points out that valid perspectives from different approaches can be combined into a new structure. One point needs reiteration: verbal dismissal of theory does not mean that theory is actually dismissed. An explicit examination of theoretical issues is, if Beutler's (1983) thesis is valid, a therapeutic factor. Unexamined theory is, as Cornsweet (1983) has shown, potentially damaging to clients.

There are other reasons for the explicit examination of theoretical issues. As the model shows, a counsellor's theory is partly determined by a number of personal factors and personal preferences. Unless the impact of these determinants is examined explicitly, eclectic counsellors are open to the criticism that they adopt a theoretical perspective that suits them personally rather than one which has any clinical utility and validity.

A final argument for eclectic counsellors making their theoretical perspectives explicit to themselves is that these perspectives are likely to have a 'for better or worse' impact on their clients. According to Bordin's (1979) concept of the therapeutic alliance, the probability of effective counselling is enhanced if counsellor and client have a shared understanding of the nature of the latter's problems. If eclectic counsellors are to communicate such understanding to their clients, a prior and explicit examination of the foundations of such understanding is necessary if inconsistent, incoherent and thus unhelpful conceptions are to be avoided. Whether, in fact, eclectic counsellors conceptualise their clients' problems from a base broader than that of other counsellors is as yet unknown.

# Developing Effective Counselling Strategies

Goldfried (1978, 1980) has argued that the most likely arena where counsellors of different persuasions may find meaningful consensus lies at a level of abstraction between theory and technique. This is the level of 'clinical strategies'. Such strategies imply principles of therapeutic change. Goldfried (1982) argues that to increase the likelihood of productive dialogue between counsellors of different persuasions, counsellors need to use a neutral language in explaining their clinical strategies, i.e. one which is free from the jargon of specific therapeutic schools. Whether this enterprise will facilitate therapeutic *rapprochement* remains to be seen, but the idea is particularly appealing to those eclectic counsellors known as integrationists. Goldfried (1980) quotes two examples of such clinical strategies, the first being that of providing the client with new corrective emotional experiences and the second being that of offering the client direct feedback. Having conceptualised clinical strategies in this way, counsellors are then faced with a number of different ways of implementing such strategies. They can best do this by using a variety of counselling methods and techniques.

A number of important points need to be made at this juncture. First, the selection of strategies is to some degree based on a counsellor's theoretical formulations, as described in the previous section. Thus, if the counsellor's strategy is to help a client modify a faulty cognition, the counsellor is operating on the assumption that faulty cognitions are involved in the client's problem and that changing it will help to overcome his or her problem. Thus, once again, eclectic counsellors cannot avoid operating on theoretical assumptions.

Secondly, eclectic counsellors are likely to pay close attention to client variability in the selection of clinical strategies. Here, Beutler's (1983) work is important, since eclectic counsellors will use different strategies dependent upon (1) the client's coping style, (2) the complexity of the client's symptoms and (3) the client's reactance level.

Thirdly, eclectic counsellors are likely to pay close attention to the stage of counselling in selecting counselling strategies (for example, McConnaughty, Prochaska and Velicer, 1983; Egan, 1990). Richert (1983) has shown that different clients require different strategies and techniques at the initial stage of counselling. Using two dimensions – an authority continuum covering issues of counsellor power and status and a counsellor orientation towards problems – he has identified four types of client on the basis of their role expectations for counsellor behaviour. *Medical modellers* are clients who prefer counsellors to be high on the authority dimension and to focus directly on problems. *Revelationists* prefer counsellors to be high in power but to scrutinise their personal feelings and experiences closely. *Problem-solvers* prefer counsellors to occupy a position of lesser authority and focus upon their problems. Finally, *explorers* want their counsellors to be companions (low authority) on a trip into their psychological space. Clearly, if counsellors are to engage all such clients productively in counselling, care has to be taken in selecting appropriate counselling strategies at the outset either to meet a particular client's role expectations or to modify them.

Fourthly, eclectic counsellors are likely to give careful consideration to the most appropriate style to adopt in implementing strategies with particular clients in accordance with their perceptions of these clients on salient dimensions (Anchin and Kiesler, 1982). Such counsellors are aware that particular counselling styles may reinforce a client's psychological problems by re-confirming negative and disturbance-perpetuating schemata, whilst other styles may provide disconfirming evidence for the client and thereby promote change: for example, adopting a very active–directive style with a very passive client may reinforce that client's passivity, whilst adopting a moderately expressive style with a client who uses intellectualisation as a defence may promote change.

Fifthly, therapeutic alliance considerations are salient here (as they are throughout the model). If counsellor and client share a common understanding as to the purpose of the counsellor's strategies, and if the client can see that the implementation of such strategies will help him or her reach his or her therapeutic goals, then the chances of productive counselling will be enhanced.

It is possible that eclectic counsellors use a broader range of strategies than do those belonging to a particular school, although this is a matter for empirical inquiry. It is likely, however, that eclectic counsellors' personal preferences will also play a role in strategy selection; but again this question awaits research. In this regard, Hill and O'Grady (1985) carried out important research which may prove valuable in promoting greater understanding of the range of strategies that eclectic counsellors employ. They studied the intentions that counsellors have which determine their responses in counselling. They asked counsellors to listen to tape recordings of counselling sessions and to check which intention(s) guided every counsellor response in the session. Whilst this method is open to the criticism of post hoc rationalisation, it is an important step forward in furthering understanding of counsellor decision-making. Table 7.1 lists 19 such counsellor intentions. It is noteworthy that Hill and O'Grady include the term 'to relieve counsellor' as an intention; this serves as another reminder that some clinical strategies may be implicitly employed to protect the counsellor rather than help the client.

Hill (personal communication) has observed that whilst these counsellor intentions can be conceptualised as referring to strategies, these strategies tend to be more immediate in focus. Therapeutic strategies, then, vary along a time–focus continuum. A strategy may be adopted for a short period of time within a session, for an entire session or even over a number of sessions. In addition, strategies may be organised hierarchically. A counsellor may implement a particular strategy to enable him or her at a later date to implement another.

# Employing Different Counselling Methods and Techniques

Having developed a set of counselling strategies to use with a particular client, the eclectic counsellor can now select from a wide range of

**Table 7.1** Counsellor intentions

| | | |
|---|---|---|
| 1 | To set limits or make arrangements | To structure, establish goals and objectives of treatment, outline methods to attain goals, correct expectations about treatment, or establish rules or parameters of relationship (e.g. time, length, fees, cancellation policies, homework content etc.) |
| 2 | To gather information | To find out specific facts about history, client functioning, future plans etc. |
| 3 | To give information | To educate, give facts, correct misperceptions or misinformation, give reasons for counsellor's behaviour or procedures |
| 4 | To support and build rapport | To provide a warm, supportive, empathic environment |
| | | To increase trust and rapport and build relationship, to help client feel accepted, understood, supported, comfortable, reassured and less anxious |
| | | To help establish a person-to-person relationship |
| 5 | To focus | To help client focus, get back on track, change subject, channel or structure if he or she is unable to begin or if he or she has been diffuse, rambling or shifting topics |
| 6 | To clarify | To provide or solicit more elaboration, emphasis or specification when client or counsellor has been vague, incomplete, confusing, contradictory or inaudible |
| 7 | To instil hope | To convey the expectation that change is possible and likely to occur and that the counsellor will be able to help the client |
| | | To restore morale |
| | | To build up the client's confidence to make changes |
| 8 | To promote relief from tension or unhappy feelings | To allow the client a chance to cathart, let go or talk through feelings and problems |
| 9 | To identify maladaptive cognitions | To point out illogical or irrational thoughts or attitudes (e.g. 'I must be perfect' etc.) |
| 10 | To identify maladaptive behaviours | To give feedback about the client's inappropriate behaviour and/or its consequences |
| | | To do a behavioural analysis |
| | | To point out games |
| 11 | To encourage a sense of self-control | To help the client own or gain a sense of control over his or her own thoughts, feelings, behaviours or impulses |
| | | To help the client become more appropriately internal rather than inappropriately external in taking responsibility for one's role |

| 12 | To identify, intensify and/or enable acceptance of feelings | To encourage understanding or provoke the client to become aware of or deepen underlying or hidden feelings or affect or to experience feelings at a deeper level |
| 13 | To stimulate insight | To encourage understanding of the underlying reasons, dynamics, assumptions or unconscious motivations for cognitions, behaviours, attitudes or feelings (may include an understanding of client's reactions to other's behaviours) |
| 14 | To build more appropriate behaviours or cognitions | To help develop new and more adaptive skills, behaviours or cognitions to inculcate new ways of dealing with self and others (maybe to instil new, more adaptive assumptive models, frameworks, explanations or conceptualisations) (Maybe to give an assessment or opinion about client functioning that will help client to see self in new way) |
| 15 | To reinforce change attempts | To give positive reinforcement on feedback about behavioural cognitive or affective attempts at change in order to enhance the probability that the change will be continued or maintained<br>To encourage risk-taking and new ways of behaving |
| 16 | To overcome obstacles to change | To analyse lack of progress, resistance or failure to adhere to therapeutic procedures, either past or possibilities of relapse in the future |
| 17 | To challenge | To jolt the client out of a present state<br>To shake up current beliefs or feelings or behaviours<br>To help client question the necessity of maintaining old patterns |
| 18 | To resolve problems in the therapeutic relationship | To deal with issues as they arise in the relationship in order to build a smooth working alliance<br>To heal ruptures in the alliance<br>To deal with dependency issues appropriate to stage in treatment<br>To uncover and resolve distortions in client's thinking about the relationship which are based on past experiences rather than current reality |
| 19 | To relieve counsellor | To protect or defend the counsellor, to take care of the counsellor's needs<br>To alleviate anxiety<br>To try unduly to persuade, argue or feel good or superior at the expense of the client |

From Clara Hill.

counselling methods and techniques to implement these strategies. A technique is a well-defined, circumscribed therapeutic manoeuvre, such as behavioural rehearsal, the two-chair technique or rational–emotive imagery, whereas a therapeutic method can be seen as a more general counselling manoeuvre, for example responding from within a client's frame of reference or the use of counsellor immediacy. It is at this point in the model that the counsellor's eclectic stance is likely to become most apparent in that he or she selects from a diverse range of counselling methods and techniques culled from different schools of counselling. Once a particular counselling strategy has been selected and agreed with the client, the counsellor can use a variety of different techniques to achieve the same therapeutic end. Another advantage of eclecticism at this stage is that the eclectic counsellor can use a variety of alternative methods and techniques if a given counselling technique or method fails. Indeed, therapeutic alliance considerations would suggest that it would be productive for counsellors to discuss with their clients the different methods and techniques that could possibly be employed to implement clinical strategies and thereby achieve therapeutic goals. Letting the client choose the most appropriate method or technique for his own particular situation would be particularly beneficial. There is, in fact, evidence that clients who receive a form of treatment for which they have expressed a preference achieve better results than do clients who receive randomly assigned or non-preferred treatment (Devine and Fernald, 1973).

It is important to observe at this stage that eclectic counsellors should distinguish between the possible short- and long-term effects of particular counselling methods and techniques. Some methods and techniques may promote short-term benefits but lead to problems later in counselling. For example, some cathartic techniques may be helpful for clients in the short term but reinforce disturbance-creating philosophies in the long term (Dryden, 1982). Judging the short- and long-term consequences of employing given methods and techniques is dependent upon: (1) knowledge of the client's personality structure and patterns, (2) one's theory of healthy functioning and disturbance and (3) outcome research.

With regard to the use of techniques and methods in eclectic counselling the following points are pertinent. First, in the same way that certain eclectic counsellors have preferences for particular counselling strategies, it is probably true that counsellors will use certain methods and techniques more frequently than others. Secondly, being sensitive to the needs of individual clients, eclectic counsellors are likely to use different ways of employing a given method or technique with different clients; the point about counselling style has already been made. However, the artistic nature of therapeutic work is also relevant here. Lazarus (1978) makes an important point in this respect, first quoted in Chapter 6, but which bears repeating:

when I select systematic desensitization as one of the techniques to be used with a given client, I do so because scientific studies have suggested that this method has a high success rate in certain instances. But the different way in which I explain its rationale to specific clients, the individual pace, manner and structure I employ with different people and the variety of ways in which I introduce scenes, embroider images, and embellish tailor-made themes, rest heavily on ... artistic skill. (p. 24)

The selection of specific methods and techniques and the way these are executed are determined not only by the above 'rational factors'; it is well known that occasionally counsellors respond to their clients in non-therapeutic ways. Countertransference factors, mood factors, the impact of certain client factors on certain counsellors and general distractions are all potential determinants that may interfere with counsellor decision-making. This is why having their counselling work supervised is highly desirable for all counsellors.

# Specific Counsellor Responses

Methods and techniques have been defined as general and specific manoeuvres respectively, used in the service of broad counselling strategies. As such they are composed of a number of discrete counsellor responses known as counsellor 'turns'. A counsellor turn is defined as everything a counsellor says between two client statements and, as can be seen from Figure 7.1, is influenced by similar factors to those impinging on the use of methods and techniques as well as by preceding client responses. When counsellor behaviour is analysed at this level, it may be difficult to detect differences between counsellors of different orientations and eclectic counsellors; yet it is at this level that counsellors have direct impact on their clients. This perhaps accounts for the therapeutic equivalence of widely different theoretical approaches to counselling.

As noted above, this level of counsellor behaviour has been studied by Hill and O'Grady (1985) with the aim of identifying counsellor intentions to implement clinical strategies. Thus although the direct study of specific counsellor responses may not help us to understand the work of eclectic counsellors, it is important to examine this level of behaviour so as to help illuminate the decision-making processes of eclectic counsellors.

In conclusion, it should be noted that the model outlined in Figure 7.1 assumes that counsellors will offer clients a minimum level of appropriate therapeutic conditions (such as empathy, genuineness and respect), and these factors should be given due consideration along with the other elements in the model when reasons for therapeutic failure are sought.

# References

ANCHIN, J.C. and KIESLER, D.J. (Eds) (1982). *Handbook of Interpersonal Psychotherapy.* New York: Pergamon.

BEUTLER, L.E. (1983). *Eclectic Psychotherapy: A systematic approach.* New York: Pergamon.

BORDIN, E.S. (1979). The generalizability of the psychoanalytic concept of the working alliance. *Psychotherapy: Theory, Research and Practice* **16**, 252–260.

CORNSWEET, C. (1983). Nonspecific factors and theoretical choice. *Psychotherapy: Theory, Research and Practice* **20**, 307–313.

DAVIS, J.D. (1983). Slaying the psychoanalytic dragon: An integrationist's commentary on Yates. *British Journal of Clinical Psychology* **22**, 133–134.

DEVINE, D.A. and FERNALD, P.S. (1973). Outcome effects of receiving a preferred, randomly assigned or nonpreferred therapy. *Journal of Consulting and Clinical Psychology* **41**: 104–107.

DRYDEN, W. (1982). Rational-emotive therapy and eclecticism. *The Counsellor* **3**(5), 15–22.

EGAN, G. (1990). *The Skilled Helper: A systematic approach to effective helping,* 4th edn. Monterey, CA: Brooks/Cole.

GARFIELD, S.L. (1980). *Psychotherapy: An eclectic approach.* New York: Wiley.

GOLDFRIED, M.R. (1978). On the search for effective intervention strategies. *The Counseling Psychologist* **7**(3), 28–30.

GOLDFRIED, M.R. (1980). Toward the delineation of therapeutic change principles. *American Psychologist* **35**, 991–999.

GOLDFRIED, M.R. (1982). On the history of therapeutic integration. *Behavior Therapy* **13**, 572–593.

HILL, C.E. and O'GRADY, K.E. (1985). List of therapist intentions illustrated in a case study and with therapists of varying theoretical orientations. *Journal of Counseling Psychology* **32**, 3–22.

LAZARUS, A.A. (1978). Science and beyond. *The Counseling Psychologist* **7**(3), 24–25.

MCCONNAUGHTY, F.A., PROCHASKA, J.O. and VELICER, W.F. (1983). Stages of change in psychotherapy: Measurement and sample profiles. *Psychotherapy: Theory, Research and Practice* **20**, 368–375.

RICHERT, A. (1983). Differential prescription for psychotherapy on the basis of client role preferences. *Psychotherapy: Theory, Research and Practice* **20**, 321–329.

STANDAL, S.W. and CORSINI, R.J. (Eds.) (1959). *Critical Incidents in Psychotherapy.* Englewood Cliffs, NJ: Prentice-Hall.

WACHTEL, P.L. (1977). *Psychoanalysis and Behavior Therapy: Toward an integration.* New York: Basic Books.

YATES, A.J. (1983). Behaviour therapy and psychodynamic psychotherapy: Basic conflict or reconciliation and integration? *British Journal of Clinical Psychology* **22**, 107–125.

# Chapter 8
# The Therapeutic Alliance in Rational–Emotive Counselling (REC)

## Bordin's Concept of the Therapeutic Alliance

As a rational–emotive counsellor I have found the work of Ed Bordin (1979) on the concept of the therapeutic alliance particularly helpful in developing a basic framework for the conduct of REC. Bordin argues that the therapeutic alliance refers to the complex of attachments and shared understandings formed and activities undertaken by counsellors and clients as the former attempt to help the latter with their psychological problems.

As discussed in Chapter 3 Bordin has stressed that there are three major components of the therapeutic alliance: (1) *bonds* – which refer to the interpersonal connectedness between counsellor and client; (2) *goals* – which refer to the aims of both counsellor and client; and (3) *tasks* – which are activities carried out by both counsellor and client in the service of the latter's goals.

I will consider each of these components separately and show that rational–emotive counsellors have important clinical decisions to make in each of the three alliance domains so as to individualise counselling for each client and thus maximise therapeutic benefit.

At the outset it should be noted that Bordin (1979) has speculated that effective counselling occurs when therapist and client (1) have an appropriately bonded working relationship; (2) mutually agree on the goals of the therapeutic enterprise; and (3) both understand their own and the other person's therapeutic tasks and agree to carry out these to implement the client's goals.

First published in 1987.

## Bonds

The major concern of rational–emotive counsellors in the bond domain should be to establish and maintain an appropriately bonded relationship that will encourage *each* individual client to implement his or her goal-directed therapeutic tasks. It should be underlined that there is no *single* effective bond that can be formed with clients in REC; different clients require different bonds. This observation became clear to me when, on a 6 months' sabbatical at the Center for Cognitive Therapy in Philadelphia in 1981, I saw two clients on the same afternoon who benefited from a different bonded relationship with me. At 4 p.m. I saw Mrs G., a 50-year-old married business woman, who was impressed with my British professional qualifications and whose responses to initial questions indicated that she anticipated and preferred a very formal relationship with her counsellor. I provided such a relationship by using formal language, citing the research literature whenever appropriate, wearing a suit, shirt and tie and by referring to myself as Dr Dryden and to my client as Mrs G. On one occasion I inadvertently used her first name and was put firmly in my place concerning the protocol of professional relationships. On another occasion I disclosed a piece of personal information in order to make a therapeutic point and was told in no uncertain terms: 'Young man, I am not paying you good money to hear about your problems.' Here, a counsellor is faced with the choice of respecting and meeting a client's bond anticipations and preferences or examining the reasons why, for example, this client was so adamantly against her counsellor's informality. In my experience the latter strategy is rarely productive and rational–emotive counsellors are recommended to fulfil their clients' preferences for counselling style as long as doing so does not reinforce the client's psychological problems.

At 5 p.m. on the same afternoon I regularly saw Mr B., a 42-year-old male nurse who indicated that he did not respond well to his previous counsellor's neutrality and formality. Our counselling sessions were thus characterized by an informal bond. Before seeing him I would remove my jacket and tie that I wore for Mrs G.; in sessions we would use our first names and would both have our feet up on my desk. We also developed the habit of taking turns to bring in cans of soda and my client referred to our meetings as 'rap sessions' while I conceptualised my work as counselling within an informal context.

I maintain that Mrs G. would not have responded well to an informal counselling relationship nor would Mr B. have done as well with a highly formal mode of counselling. Thus, I argue that it is important that rational–emotive counsellors pay attention to the question: 'Which bond is likely to be most effective with a particular client at a given time in the therapeutic process?' Drawing upon social psychological principles, certain writers have argued that some clients show more progress when the therapeutic bond is based on liking and trustworthiness, whilst others flourish more when the bond emphasises counsellor credibility and expertness (Strong and Claiborn, 1982; Beutler, 1983; Dorn, 1984). Future research in REC could fruitfully address the issue of which bond is effective with which clients. However, until we have such data, counsellors could make decisions about which type of bond to foster on the basis of an early assessment of the client's anticipations and preferences in the bond domain and to try to meet such expectations, at least initially. This is one reason why I would caution novice counsellors against emulating the counselling style of leading REC practitioners whose bond with clients may be based mainly on prestige and expertness. Rational–emotive counsellors should thus be prepared to emphasise different aspects of themselves with different clients in the bond domain, without adopting an inauthentic facade, and to monitor transactions in this domain throughout counselling.

How can this best be done? One way would be to administer a modified portion of Lazarus's (1981) Life History Questionnaire which focuses on client's expectations regarding counselling. The items: 'How do you think a counsellor should interact with his or her clients?' and 'What personal qualities do you think the ideal counsellor should possess?' are particularly relevant and could usefully provide impetus for further exploration of this issue at the outset of counselling. If the client has had counselling previously, the current counsellor could usefully explore which aspects of the previous counsellor(s') interactive style and behaviour were deemed by the client to be both helpful and unhelpful. Particular emphasis should be placed on the exploration of the instrumental nature of previous therapeutic bonds since statements such as 'He was warm and caring' are of little use unless the client evaluated these qualities positively and attributed therapeutic progress to these factors.

Furthermore, and for similar reasons, I have found it helpful to explore clients' accounts of people in their lives who have had both positive and negative therapeutic influence on their personal development. Such exploration may provide the counsellor with important clues concerning which types of therapeutic bonds to promote actively with certain clients and which bonds to avoid developing with others.

Counselling style is another aspect of the bond domain which requires attention. Interpersonally orientated counsellors (e.g. Anchin and Kiesler, 1982) have argued that practitioners need to be aware that therapeutic styles have a 'for better or worse' impact on different clients. Rational–emotive counsellors tend to be active and directive in their style of conducting counselling. This counselling style may not be entirely productive with both passive clients and, as Beutler (1983) has argued, clients who are highly reactive to interpersonal influence. Clients who tend to be passive in their interpersonal style of relating may 'pull' an increasingly active style from their counsellors who may in turn reinforce these clients' passivity with their increased activity. Clients whose psychological problems are intrinsically bound up with a passive style of relating are particularly vulnerable in this regard. It is important that rational–emotive counsellors need to engage their clients productively at a level which constructively encourages increased activity on their part but without threatening them through the use of an *overly* passive style of practising REC.

Beutler (1983) has argued that all approaches to counselling can be viewed as a process of persuasion and this is particularly true of REC practitioners who aim to 'persuade' clients to re-evaluate and change their irrational beliefs. As such, rational–emotive counsellors need to be especially careful in working with clients for whom such persuasive attempts may be perceived as especially threatening (i.e. highly reactant clients). Here it is important that counsellors execute their strategies with due regard to helping such clients to preserve their sense of autonomy, emphasising throughout that these clients are in control of their own thought processes and decisions concerning whether or not to change them. At present, the above suggestions are speculative and await full empirical inquiry, but my clinical work has led me to question the desirability of establishing the same therapeutic bond with all clients and of practising rational–emotive counselling in an unchanging therapeutic style.

## Goals

The major concern of rational–emotive counsellors in the goal domain of the alliance is to ensure that there is agreement between counsellor and client on the client's outcome goals for change. A prerequisite of such agreement concerns client and counsellor arriving at a shared understanding of the client's most relevant problems as defined by the client (Meichenbaum and Gilmore, 1982). Difficulties may occur here when the counsellor uncritically accepts the client's initial accounts of his or her problem since such accounts may well be biased by the client's internalised values, e.g. the views of significant others in the client's life. In addition, although most rational–emotive counsellors consider that early goal-setting with the client is important, clients' initial statements about their goals for change may well be coloured by their psychological disturbance as well as by their internalised values concerning what these goals *should* be. Rational–emotive counsellors need to walk a fine line between uncritically accepting clients' initial goals for change and disregarding them altogether. A helpful solution here involves establishment and maintenance of a channel of communication between client and counsellor which deals with meta-counselling issues (i.e. issues concerning matters relating to counselling itself). I have referred to the activities that occur within this channel as involving negotiations and renegotiations about therapeutic issues (see Chapter 5). Rational–emotive counsellors need to take the main responsibility for keeping this communication channel open in order to monitor clients' goals over time and to determine the reasons for shifts in these goals.

Pinsof and Catherall (1986) have made the important point that clients' goals occur (implicitly or explicitly) in reference to their most important relationships and their counsellors need to be mindful of the impact that these systems are likely to have on both the selection of such goals and the client's degree of progress towards goal attainment. Adopting this focus may well possibly mean involving parts of the client's interpersonal system in counselling itself. It also suggests that future theorising in REC could profitably assign a more central role to interpersonal issues (compare Safran, 1984; Kwee and Lazarus, 1986).

## Tasks

Rational–emotive practitioners tend to subscribe to the following coun-selling process. Initially, having agreed to offer help to the client, the counsellor attempts to structure the therapeutic process for the client and begins both to assess his or her problems in rational–emotive terms and also to help the client to view his or her problems within this framework. Goals are elicited based on a rational–emotive assessment and counselling strategies and techniques are implemented to effect the desired changes. Finally, obstacles to client change are analysed and, it is hoped, overcome, and therapeutic gains are stabilised and maintained.

Counsellors have tasks to execute at each stage in the rational–emotive counselling process and these will now be outlined.

### Structuring

Effective REC depends in part on each participant clearly understanding their respective responsibilities in the therapeutic endeavour and upon each agreeing to discharge these responsibilities in the form of carrying out counselling tasks. It is the counsellor's major responsibility to help the client to make sense of this process by providing an overall structure of mutual responsibilities and tasks. It is important to stress that structuring occurs throughout counselling and not just at the outset of the process. Sensitive counsellors who pay attention to alliance issues will structure the process using language which the client can understand and analogies which make sense to each individual person. Thus, it is often helpful to discover clients' hobbies and interests so that apt and personally meaningful structuring statements can be made. Thus, if a client is interested in golf, ascertaining how that person learned the game may be valuable in drawing parallels between the processes of learning coping skills and learning golfing skills. Both involve practice and failures can be realistically anticipated in each activity.

### Assessment and conceptualisation of clients' problems

During the assessment process, rational–emotive counsellors traditionally attempt to gain a full understanding of the cognitive and behavioural variables that are maintaining their clients' problems. During this stage two issues become salient from an alliance theory perspective. First, it is important for counsellor and client to arrive at a shared *definition* of the client's problems (i.e. what these problems are). Secondly, As Meichenbaum and Gilmore (1982) have noted, it is important for them to negotiate a shared *conceptualisation* of the client's problems (i.e. an explanation of what accounts for the existence of these problems) so that they can work productively together in the intervention stage of counselling.

When working towards shared problem conceptualisation, I argue that it is important for REC practitioners to use, wherever possible, the client's own language and concepts, particularly when providing alternative explanations of their problems. This helps counsellors to work within the range of what clients will accept as plausible conceptualisations of their problems. If clients' own ideas about the origins of their problems and more particularly what maintain them are ignored, then they may well resist accepting their counsellors' conceptualisations. As Golden (1985) has noted, sometimes counsellors often have to accept initially, for pragmatic purposes, a client's different (i.e. to the counsellor's) conceptualisation of his or her problems in order to arrive later at a shared one. In addition, rational–emotive counsellors may well privately (i.e. to themselves) conceptualise a client's problems in rational–emotive terms (irrational beliefs) while publicly (to the client) using the client's conceptualisation (e.g. negative self-hypnosis). To what extent the effectiveness of REC is based on negotiation or on the unilateral persuasion attempts of the therapist is a matter for future empirical inquiry.

### Change tactics

Once the counsellor and client have come to a mutually agreed understanding of the client's problems, the counsellor then discusses with the client a variety of techniques that the client can use to reach his or her goals. Here it is important to realise that both client and counsellor have tasks to execute.

Effective REC in the task domain tends to occur when:

1. Clients understand what their tasks are.

2. Clients understand how executing their tasks will help them achieve their goals.
3. Clients are, in fact, capable of executing their tasks and believe that they have this capability.
4. Clients understand that change comes about through repeated execution of their tasks.
5. Clients understand the tasks of their counsellors and can see the link between their counsellors' tasks, their own tasks and their goals.
6. Counsellors adequately prepare their clients to understand and execute the latter's tasks.
7. Counsellors effectively execute their tasks (i.e. they are skilled in the techniques of REC) and use a wide range of techniques appropriately.
8. Counsellors employ techniques which are congruent with their clients' learning styles. Whilst some clients learn best through action, others learn best through reading bibliotherapy texts etc.
9. Counsellors employ techniques that clients have selected (from a range of possible procedures) rather than unilaterally selecting techniques without client participation.
10. Counsellors pace their interventions appropriately.
11. Counsellors employ techniques which are potent enough to help clients achieve their goals (e.g. using exposure methods with clients with agoraphobic problems – Emmelkamp, Kuipers and Eggeraat, 1978).

# Failures in REC

I have been practising REC now for over 10 years in a variety of settings, I have worked in (1) a university counselling service; (2) a general practice; (3) a National Health Service psychiatric clinic; (4) a local marriage guidance council, and (5) private practice. I have seen, in these settings a wide range of moderately to severely disturbed individuals who were deemed to be able to benefit from weekly counselling. Whilst I do not have any hard data to substantiate the point, I have found rational–emotive counselling to be a highly effective method of individual counselling with a wide range of client problems.

However, I have of course had my therapeutic failures, and I would like, in this final section, to outline some of the factors that in my opinion have accounted for these failures. I will again use Bordin's (1979) useful concept of the therapeutic working alliance as a framework in this respect.

## Goals

I have generally been unsuccessful with clients who have devoutly clung to goals where changes in other people were desired. (In this regard, I have also failed to involve these others in counselling.) I have not been able to show or to persuade these clients that they make themselves emotionally disturbed and that it would be better if they were to work to change themselves before attempting to negotiate changes in their relationships with others. It is the devoutness of their beliefs which seems to me to be the problem here.

## Bonds

Unlike the majority of counsellors of my acquaintance, I do not regard the relationship between counsellor and client to be the sine qua non of effective counselling. I strive to accept my clients as fallible human beings and am prepared to work concertedly to help them overcome their problems, but do not endeavour to form very close, warm relationships with them. In the main, my clients do not appear to want such a relationship with me (preferring to become close and intimate with their significant others). However, occasionally I get clients who do wish to become (non-sexually) intimate with me. Some of these clients (who devoutly believe they need my love) leave counselling disappointed after I have failed to get them to give up their dire need for love or refused to give them what they think they need.

## Tasks

In this analysis I will assume throughout that counsellors are practising REC effectively and thus the emphasis will be on client variables.

My basic thesis here is that when counsellor and client agree concerning (1) the view of psychological disturbance as stated in rational–emotive theory, (2) the rational–emotive view on the acquisition and perpetuation of psychological disturbance, and (3) the rational–emotive view of therapeutic change, such agreements are likely to enhance good counselling outcome. Furthermore, the greater the disagreement between the two participants on such matters, the greater the threat that exists to the therapeutic alliance with all the negative implications that this has for good therapeutic outcome. I should say at the outset that this hypothesis has yet to be tested and should thus be viewed sceptically.

I will illustrate my points by using clinical examples from my experience as a counsellor.

### Conceptualisation of psychological disturbance

Rational–emotive theory states that much psychological disturbance can be attributed to clients' devout, absolutistic evaluations (irrational beliefs) about themselves, other people and life events. REC practitioners assume that most clients do not enter counselling sharing this viewpoint and, thus, one of the counsellor's major tasks is to persuade the client to adopt this viewpoint if effective REC is to ensue. Of course, not all clients will be so persuaded because they have their own (different) ideas about the nature of their psychological problems and what causes them and are not prepared to relinquish these. In my experience, the following clients are not good candidates for REC unless they change their ideas about the determinants of their problems: those who believe that their problems are caused by (1) external events (including events that happened in childhood), (2) physical, dietary or biochemical factors, (3) repressed basic human impulses, (4) fate or astrological factors and (5) blockages in the body.

I once had a referral from a social worker who confused REC with Reichian therapy. The client specifically wanted to work on his character armour blockages which he considered were at the source of his problems. I explained that an error had been made and that I was a rational–emotive counsellor and gave him a brief outline of the rational–emotive view of his problems. He responded with incredulity, saying that he hadn't heard such intellectualised clap-trap in a long while and asked me whether I knew of anyone who could really help him. I referred him to a local bioenergetics therapist who, apparently, helped him considerably.

### Acquisition and perpetuation of psychological disturbance

Rational–emotive theory de-emphasises the value of understanding acquisition variables in helping clients change. Rather, it stresses the importance of understanding how people perpetuate their psychological problems. This is because the theory hypothesises that whilst past events may well have contributed to clients' psychological disturbance, these did not make them disturbed, since people bring their tendency to make themselves disturbed to these events and experiences. Thus, clients who come to counselling in order to trace their psychological problems back to their roots tend not to benefit greatly from the present-centred and future-orientated focus of REC. Clients who are prepared to look for and challenge their currently held irrational beliefs do much better in REC than clients who are preoccupied with discovering how they came to hold such beliefs in the first place.

A 60-year-old woman with agoraphobic problems was firmly convinced that the origins of her panic lay in buried childhood feelings towards her parents, who while kindly disposed to my client, had placed undue burdens on her as a child. Not only did we have different views concerning the 'cause' of her present problems, but we differed as to the most appropriate time focus for the counselling. I did discuss her childhood with her, but as a stimulus to help her re-focus on her present disturbance-perpetuating beliefs, but to no avail. She quit counselling with me and started consulting a Jungian counsellor who has seen her now for 2 years with little impact on her panic disorder.

## Views on therapeutic change

REC can be viewed as a counselling system which has a 'Protestant Ethic' view of therapeutic change. Clients are urged to 'work and practise' their way to emotional health by using a variety of cognitive, emotive and behavioural methods designed to help them to change their irrational beliefs. Clients who are not prepared to put in the necessary hard work usually have less successful therapeutic outcomes than clients who challenge repeatedly their irrational beliefs in thought, feeling and deed.

It follows from the above that REC places most emphasis on the activities that clients initiate and sustain outside counselling as the major agent of change. Clients who consider that change will occur primarily from counselling sessions usually do not gain as much from REC as clients who are in accord with the rational–emotive viewpoint on this matter.

During my 6 months stay at the Center for Cognitive Therapy in Philadelphia, I saw briefly a client who had heard of cognitive therapy for depression and wished to try it. I was learning this approach at the time and was keen to do it 'by the book'. The client had recently moved to Philadelphia from Los Angeles where she had consulted an experiential therapist with whom she had had a very close relationship which, in my opinion, had encouraged her to be more dependent on love and approval than she was before she consulted him. The client had come to believe that therapeutic change depended on a very warm, close therapeutic relationship in which completing homework assignments and 'Daily Record of Dysfunctional Thoughts' sheets had no place. Despite my attempts to change her views on such matters, she left cognitive therapy to seek another experiential therapist.

## Ellis's study on failure in REC

Ellis (1983) has published some interesting data which tend to corroborate my own experiences of therapeutic failure in REC. He chose 50 of his clients who were seen in individual and/or group REC and were rated by him, and where appropriate by his associate group counsellor, as 'failures'. In some ways, this sample consisted of fairly ideal REC clients in that they were individuals (1) of above average or of superior intelligence (in Ellis's judgement and that of their other group therapist); (2) who seemed really to understand REC and who were often effective (especially in group counselling) in helping others to learn and use it; (3) who in some ways made therapeutic progress and felt that they benefited by having REC but who still retained one or more serious presenting symptoms, such as severe depression, acute anxiety, overwhelming hostility or extreme lack of self-discipline; and (4) who had at least 1 year of individual and/or group REC sessions, and sometimes considerably more.

This group was compared to clients who were selected on the same four criteria but who seemed to benefit greatly from REC. While a complete account of this study – which, of course, has its methodological flaws – can be found in Ellis (1983), the following results are most pertinent:

1. In its cognitive aspects, REC emphasises the persistent use of reason, logic and the scientific method to uproot clients' irrational beliefs. Consequently, it ideally requires intelligence, concentration and high-level, consistent cognitive self-disputation and self-persuasion. These therapeutic behaviours would tend to be disrupted or blocked by extreme disturbance, by lack of organisation, by grandiosity, by organic disruption and by refusal to do REC-type disputing of irrational ideas. All these characteristics proved to be present in significantly more failures than in those clients who responded favourably to REC.

2. REC also, to be quite successful, involves clients' forcefully and emotively changing their beliefs and actions, and their being stubbornly determined to accept responsibility for their own inappropriate feelings and vigorously work at changing these feelings (Ellis and Abrahms, 1978; Ellis and Whiteley, 1979). But the failure clients in this study were significantly more angry than those who responded well to REC; more of them were severely depressed and inactive, they were more often grandiose, and they were more frequently stubbornly resistant and rebellious. All these characteristics would presumably tend to interfere with the kind of emotive processes and changes that REC espouses.

3. REC strongly advocates that clients, in order to improve, do in vivo activity homework assignments, deliberately force themselves to engage in many painful activities until they become familiar and unpainful, and notably work and practise its multimodal techniques. But the group of clients who signally failed in this study showed abysmally low frustration tolerance, had serious behavioural addictions, led disorganised lives, refrained from doing their activity homework assignments, were more frequently psychotic and generally refused to work at therapy. All these characteristics, which were found significantly more frequently than were found on the clients who responded quite well to REC, would tend to interfere with the behavioural methods or REC.

Thus it appears from the above analysis that the old adage of counselling applies to REC: namely that clients who could most use counselling are precisely those individuals whose disturbance interferes with their benefiting from it.

# References

ANCHIN, J.C. and KIESLER, D.J. (Eds.) (1982). *Handbook of Interpersonal Psychotherapy*. New York: Pergamon.

BEUTLER, L.E. (1983). *Eclectic Psychotherapy. A systematic approach*. New York: Pergamon.

BORDIN, E.S. (1979). The generalizability of the psychoanalytic concept of the working alliance. *Psychotherapy: Theory, Research and Practice* 16, 252–260.

DORN, F.J. (1984). *Counseling as Applied Social Psychology: An introduction to the social influence model*. Springfield, IL: Thomas.

ELLIS, A. (1983). Failures in rational–emotive therapy. In Foa, E.B. and Emmelkamp, P.M.G. (Eds.) *Failures in Behavior Therapy*. New York: Wiley.

ELLIS, A. and ABRAHMS, E. (1978). *Brief Psychotherapy in Medical and Health Practice*. New York: Springer.

ELLIS, A. and WHITELEY, J.M. (Eds.) (1979). *Theoretical and Empirical Foundations of Rational–Emotive Therapy*. Monterey, CA: Brooks/Cole.

EMMELKAMP, P.M.G., KUIPERS, A.C.M. and EGGERAAT, J.B. (1978). Cognitive modification versus prolonged exposure in vivo: A comparison with agorophobics as subjects. *Behaviour Research and Therapy* 16, 33–41.

GOLDEN, W.L. (1985). An integration of Ericksonian and cognitive–behavioral hypnotherapy in the treatment of anxiety disorders. In Dowd, E.T. and Healy, J.M. (Eds.) *Case Studies in Hypnotherapy*. New York: Guilford.

KWEE, M.G.T. and LAZARUS, A.A. (1986). Multimodal therapy: The cognitive behavioural tradition and beyond. In Dryden, W. and Golden, W.L. (Eds.) *Cognitive–Behavioural Approaches to Psychotherapy*. London: Harper & Row.

LAZARUS, A.A. (1981). *The Practice of Multimodal Therapy*. New York: McGraw-Hill.

MEICHENBAUM, D. and GILMORE, J.B. (1982). Resistance from a cognitive behavioral perspective. In Wachtel, P.L. (Ed.) *Resistance*. New York: Plenum.

PINSOF, W.M. and CATHERALL, D.R. (1986). The integrative psychotherapy alliance: Family, couple, and individual scales. *Journal of Marital and Family Therapy* 12, 137–151.

SAFRAN, J.D. (1984). Assessing the cognitive-interpersonal circle. *Cognitive Therapy and Research* 8, 333–347.

STRONG, S.R. and CLAIBORN, C.D. (1982). *Change through Interaction*. New York: Wiley-Interscience.

# Chapter 9
# Rational–Emotive Counselling and Eclecticism

Eclecticism has been defined as 'consisting of that which has been selected from diverse sources, systems or styles' (*American Heritage Dictionary of the English Language*, 1971) and much has been recently written on eclectic approaches in psychotherapy (e.g. Lazarus, 1976; Shostrom, 1976; Dryden, 1980a; Garfield, 1980). However, there have been few attempts to clarify the decisions that clinicians make in broadening their therapeutic repertoire by selecting from diverse therapeutic orientation. The aim of this chapter is to show what guides rational–emotive counsellors in such endeavours.

Rational–emotive theory states that much emotional disturbance stems from the faulty inferences and irrational evaluations that clients make in endeavouring to make sense of themselves, other people and the world (Wessler and Wessler, 1980). Examples of faulty inferences have been detailed by Beck *et al.* (1979) and include arbitrary inferences, overgeneralisations and selective abstractions. Irrational evaluations are based on a philosophy of demandingness which hinders clients from achieving their long-term goals and restricts their opportunities to live effectively and creatively in the world. Such demands are couched in terms of musts, shoulds, oughts and have to's, i.e. absolutistic demands on self, others and the world. The major task of rational–emotive counsellors is to help clients correct their faulty inferences and to replace their demanding philosophy with a desiring philosophy, i.e. one which is characterised by wants, preferences and wishes. To achieve their basic task, rational–emotive counsellors focus on cognitive, affective and behavioural factors and consequently REC has been described as a comprehensive system of counselling (Ellis and Abrahms, 1978).

Rational–emotive counsellors then are guided by a particular theory of emotional disturbance and personality change (Ellis, 1978) and thus can

---

First published in 1982.

be contrasted with eclectic counsellors who de-emphasise theory (e.g. Lazarus, 1976). Theory is considered important by rational–emotive counsellors for a number of reasons. First, theory provides testable propositions for empirical study. Secondly, as Frank (1970) has shown theory helps counsellors gain emotional support from others with similar views and thus helps sustain the counsellor's morale. The third and most important reason is that theory helps guide counsellors in their work, helps them correctly select particular therapeutic procedures and gives them a framework for determining the consequences of such procedures.

# Counselling Practice

In the execution of their major task – affecting cognitive change – rational–emotive counsellors attempt to engage clients in a concrete and situationally based exploration of their problems. To encourage concreteness, counsellors tend to use explicitly or implicitly an ABCDE framework in exploring their clients' problems. Point 'A' in the framework represents an event or the clients' perceptions and inferences concerning that event. 'B' represents the client's beliefs or evaluations about the phenomenal event, whilst 'C' stands for the emotional and behavioural consequences of the client's beliefs. At point 'D' the counsellor's task is to help the client challenge his faulty inferences and irrational evaluations and replace them with more realistic and rational cognitions which leads to emotional and behavioural change at point 'E'.

In practice rational–emotive counsellors tend to start at point 'C'. The major goal here is to help clients acknowledge their feelings (without dwelling on them) and to identify their actions. In doing so the counsellor may very well use procedures derived from other counselling systems. For example, if a client experiences difficulty in acknowledging feelings, the rational–emotive counsellor might employ a gestalt awareness exercise or psychodramatic technique with the specific purpose at this stage of encouraging the client to acknowledge feelings.

After helping the client to identify correctly emotional and behavioural responses, the counsellor shifts his or her attention to the context in which such responses arise (point A). Exploration at this point involves the counsellor paying attention to the client's description of the relevant context. The client is helped to describe his perception of the relevant situation fairly briefly. The counsellor tends not to dwell upon those events and discourages the client from presenting too many or problem-irrelevant contexts. The goal of the counsellor is to aid the client in adequately framing the problem so that she can assist in the identification and correction of presently held faulty inferences and beliefs. In practice the context tends to be either one that is anticipated or one of recent occurrence and thus REC tends to be a present and future-oriented approach to counselling. Rational–emotive counsellors tend not to focus on events that have occurred in the distant past since it is argued that such exploration does not aid the correction of presently held faulty cognitions (Ellis, 1962). However, Dryden (1979) has found that in certain circumstances such exploration does assist the counsellor in his or her dissuasion strategies with some clients. Thus understanding the likely origins of presently held beliefs may motivate such clients to change such beliefs. The point at issue here is that the purpose of exploring such past events is to facilitate the disputing of *presently* held inferences and beliefs.

At point B in the ABCDE framework, the counsellor's task is to help the client identify the irrational evaluations that the latter employs in appraising the relevant context. Here the counsellor is not limited to verbal interventions such as: 'What are you saying to yourself?', that are often seen in counselling transcripts. In fact, in the author's experience a common answer to such questions is – 'nothing'. In addition to psychodrama (Nardi, 1979) and gestalt methods, various role-playing and imagery methods may be used as an aid to facilitate the discovery of irrational beliefs. Indeed, person-centred procedures for some patients may be employed. Such clients find the less active–directive style implicit in such procedures helpful in exploring and discovering meanings and beliefs (DiLoreto, 1971). Rather than abandon REC for person-centred counselling, an eclectic rational–emotive counsellor would vary her therapeutic style but not the theoretical underpinnings of her system.

Point D in the framework is also called the dissuasion process (Wessler and Wessler, 1980). On attempting to dissuade the client, the counsellor may use a wide variety of cognitive, imaginal, affective and behavioural methods, and may suggest similar procedures for the patient to use between sessions as the latter strives to put into practice in everyday life what he or she has learned in counselling (point E).

# Theory-inspired Guidelines for Choosing Appropriate Counselling Procedures

Thus far it has been argued that rational–emotive counsellors may choose from a range of cognitive, experiential and behavioural methods to facilitate their task of working within the ABCDE framework. However, rational–emotive counsellors are mindful of possible negative effects of employing certain procedures and by no means would employ all available procedures. There are a number of issues that rational–emotive counsellors have in mind when deciding whether or not to employ a particular therapeutic procedure.

## Helping clients get better rather than feel better

One basic aim of rational–emotive counsellors is to promote long-term philosophically based change as opposed to helping clients feel better in the short term. Thus rational–emotive counsellors may deliberately avoid being unduly warm towards their clients and would be wary of employing cathartic methods. The hazard of undue counsellor warmth is that it may lead to increased long-term dependence in a client who may then believe that they are worth while because the counsellor is acting very warmly towards them. However, if the counsellor or other significant people act coldly towards the client, he or she may then conclude that he or she is worthless. Thus, undue counsellor warmth, although clients feel better when so exposed, tends to distract them from dealing with the more difficult task of accepting themselves unconditionally (Ellis, 1977). For this reason an intense relationship between counsellor and client is generally avoided. The counsellor strives to accept the client as a fallible human being without being unduly warm towards him or her.

Cathartic methods have the short-term value of encouraging relief of pent-up feelings, but in the long term, if not employed sparingly and briefly, often encourage clients to practise their already well-ingrained irrational philosophies. For example, cathartic procedures which place emphasis on the ventilation of intense angry feelings (e.g. pounding a cushion) run the risk of encouraging processes of blaming which are, according to rational–emotive theory, a feature of the irrational philosophy underlying anger. Rational–emotive counsellors might employ such procedures when they wish to help clients to acknowledge their feelings, but the client would then be quickly encouraged to consider the philosophy underlying such feelings.

## Self-esteem vs self-acceptance

In REC, self-esteem is defined as a form of global self-rating and is to be avoided since according to rational–emotive theory it has problematic long-term implications for clients. Procedures based on self-esteem notions encourage clients to define themselves as worth while or competent so long as they gain approval or succeed at valued tasks. They are thus prone to defining themselves as worthless and incompetent if they receive disapproval or fail at the same task. Furthermore, rational–emotive theory states that it is nonsensical to give humans global ratings since they are on-going, complex, ever-changing organisms who defy such ratings. As an alternative, rational–emotive counsellors not only endeavour to get clients accepting themselves as on-going, complex, ever-changing fallible human beings but also encourage them to rate their traits, aspects and behaviour but not their selves. Many procedures do not in fact discourage clients from making such global self-ratings. For example, many counsellors give clients homework assignments which are designed to encourage the client to succeed. Thus a client who succeeds at approaching a woman at a discotheque may conclude that because he has been able to do this, perhaps he is not worthless after all. The implication would be that if he failed in his assignment then this would be a confirmation of his worthlessness. Rational–emotive counsellors, by contrast, may at times encourage clients to deliberately go out and fail since such a failure experience presents them with opportunities to work on accepting themselves as fallible humans rather than subhumans when they fail. In reality, rational–emotive counsellors suggest both success and failure-oriented homework assignments to their clients.

## Anger vs annoyance

Rational–emotive theory clearly distinguishes between anger and annoyance. Annoyance results when something occurs which we view as a trespass on our personal conceptual domain, which we strongly dislike but which we refrain from demanding should not have happened. There is an absence of blaming of self, other or the world for the deed, i.e. the deed is rated but the perpetrator of the deed is accepted. In contrast anger stems from the jehovian demand that the trespass absolutely should not have occurred and the trespasser is damnable. Counsellors from other persuasions often do not make such a clear distinction and thus the counselling procedures which they employ may encourage the full expression and ventilation of anger rather than annoyance. If this occurs then rational–emotive counsellors would avoid using these procedures. As mentioned earlier, whilst the full expression and ventilation of anger helps the person feel better it often encourages adherence to a long-term and damaging anger-creating philosophy. In REC procedures are used to help clients to fully acknowledge their anger but then they are encouraged to dispute the underlying philosophy.

## Desensitisation vs implosion

Rational–emotive counsellors face a choice of two different approaches when the issue of suggesting homework assignments to clients arises. They can either suggest that clients gradually face their fears and overcome their problems in a slow stepwise fashion while minimising discomfort (desensitisation), or they can suggest that clients take a risk and forcefully confront their fears and their problems while tolerating discomfort (implosion). Rational–emotive counsellors very definitely favour implosion-based assignments since they help clients overcome their 'low frustration tolerance' (LFT) or 'discomfort anxiety', constructs which, according to rational–emotive theory, play a central role in preventing change (Ellis, 1980). Consequently such counsellors would avoid helping patients to overcome gradually and painlessly their problems because such procedures are viewed as encouraging patients to cling to their philosophy of LFT which actually decreases their chances of maintaining therapeutic improvement and increases the possibility of relapse (Ellis, 1980).

Due to the somewhat unusual stance taken on the above issues rational–emotive counselling has proved rather difficult to combine with other methods derived from different theoretical origins. Garfield and Kurtz (1977) make a similar observation, noting in their study of 154 clinicians' eclectic views that REC was occasionally combined with learning theory-based approaches but was not combined with psychoanalytical, neo-analytical, person-centered, humanistic or Sullivanian orientations.

# Counselling Style

Ellis (1976) speaking for rational–emotive theory argues that humans have great difficulty maintaining the changes that they make more easily in the short term because of the strong biological basis to irrational thinking. Because of this difficulty, Ellis urges rational–emotive counselling to adopt an active–directive, forceful and persistent counselling style and also encourage their clients to be equally active, forceful and persistent with themselves. However, is such a style beneficial with a wide range of clients? Or should rational–emotive counsellors vary their counselling style with different clients? If the latter is to be advised, what criteria should be employed to assist rational–emotive counsellors in these important decisions?

The first question remains unanswered since there is a lack of research which has systematically studied the effects of active–directive REC across a wide range of clients. There is, however, some research evidence concerning different counselling styles with different clients which has relevance for REC practitioners. DiLoreto (1971) in a study using socially anxious clients found that active–directive REC was more effective with introverts than with extroverts in the sample whilst person-centred counselling was more effective with extroverts. This suggests that REC practitioners might effectively adopt a less directive, more reflective style of REC, when working with socially anxious extroverts. Morley and Watkins (1974) carried out a treatment study with speech anxious patients. They found that active–directive REC benefited external locus of control clients most, whilst internal locus of control patients profited most from a modified REC approach where rational and irrational beliefs relevant to speech anxiety were merely presented and not challenged in the usual fashion. To what extent these findings can be generalised to other client populations remains unclear. We must also wait for studies to consider Ellis's point often made in practice that the stronger clients adhere to irrational philosophies the more forceful the counsellor had better be.

Carson (1969) advocates an interpersonally based system to help the counsellor vary his or her interpersonal style according to the client's own style. Unproductive interlocking interactional patterns arise when the counsellor adopts a manner of relating which confirms the client in his own self-defeating style. The counsellor's task is to adopt an interpersonal style which (1) does not reinforce the client's dysfunctional style and (2) provides a disconfirming experience for the client. For example, with a passive client, it would be important for the rational–emotive counsellor to refrain from adopting a very active style which might reinforce the client's self-defeating passivity.

Thus, rational–emotive counsellors had better be mindful of Eschenroeder's (1979) question: 'Which therapeutic style is most effective with what kind of client?' (p. 5).

## Therapeutic Modalities

Rational–emotive theory holds that the important modalities of human experience – cognitive (verbal and imaginal), affective and behavioural – are overlapping rather than separate systems (Ellis, 1962). However, it may be important for REC practitioners to vary the emphasis they place in working within the various modalities with different clients. What criteria might be important as guides to decision-making in this area bearing in mind that the ultimate goal is a common one (i.e. to effect philosophical changes)? One set of criteria might be the ability of clients to handle verbal concepts. The author's own experience of working as a counselling psychologist in a working-class region is that with those clients who find it difficult using words it is important for counsellors to focus on the behavioural modality both within and between sessions. When teaching rational concepts, important with such patients, then it is essential to use the visual mode of communication as an adjunct to the verbal mode. Thus, I use pen and paper a lot, sketching diagrams to facilitate such clients' understanding of difficult rational concepts. In addition, I have devised a number of visual models to illustrate rational concepts (Dryden, 1980b). When clients employ words to protect them from emotional experience, i.e. when they employ intellectualisation as a major defensive style, then rational–emotive counsellors might more effectively focus on the experiential modality helping such clients to acquaint themselves with that mode of experience from which they have shielded themselves. If counsellors spend too much time engaging such clients in traditional rational–emotive socratic dialogue then they may well reinforce their clients' defensive style. Such speculations of course need to be tested.

Beutler (1979) has suggested a system which combines therapeutic modalities and styles in determining whether certain approaches to counselling are more effective than others with clients on three major client dimensions. The first dimension is symptom complexity. If symptoms are circumscribed Beutler (1979) hypothesises that a greater behavioural focus would be more effective, whereas if they are more complex a greater cognitive focus is needed. The second dimension is defensive style: with client with an external defensive style, the counsellor needs to emphasise the behavioural modality in counselling whereas cognitive interventions are required with clients utilising an internal defensive style. The third dimension taps the degree to which external events are construed as representing a threat to the person's autonomy-reactance. If the client is high on the reactance dimension, i.e. if he or she is predisposed to view external events as autonomy-endangering, then the counsellor would be more productive if he or she adopted a less directive, more experiential, counselling style. If the client is low on this dimension then greater counsellor direction with a more behavioural focus is needed. Beutler (1979) reviewed empirical studies relevant to his hypotheses but found only meagre to moderate support for these hypotheses. However, these hypotheses were not tested directly and Beutler's system remains a promising one in that it provides the rational–emotive counsellor with some guidelines as to possible variations in style and modality focus with different clients.

In conclusion, it has been shown how REC practitioners employ rational–emotive theory as a guide in their choice of a wide array of counselling interventions. In addition, the argument was advanced that REC practitioners are advised to take into account client characteristics in making decisions concerning counselling style and modality-focus. However, the central purpose of the eclectic REC practitioner remains the modification of faulty inferences and irrational beliefs.

# References

*American Heritage Dictionary of the English Language* (1971). New York: American Heritage.

BECK, A.T., RUSH, A.J., SHAW, B.F. and EMERY, G. (1979). *Cognitive Therapy of Depression.* New York: Wiley.

BEUTLER, L.E. (1979). Toward specific psychological therapies for specific conditions. *Journal of Consulting and Clinical Psychology* 47, 882–897.

CARSON, R.C. (1969). *Interaction Concepts of Personality.* London: George Allen & Unwin.

DiLORETO, A.E. (1971). *Comparative Psychotherapy: An experimental analysis.* Chicago: Aldine-Atherton.

DRYDEN, W. (1979). Past messages and disputations: the client and significant others. *Rational Living* 14(1), 26–28.

DRYDEN, W. (1980a). 'Eclectic' approaches in individual counselling: some pertinent issues. *The Counsellor* 3, 24–30.

DRYDEN, W. (1980b). Nightmares and fun. Paper given at the Third National Conference on Rational–Emotive Therapy, June, New York.

ELLIS, A. (1962). *Reason and Emotion in Psychotherapy*. New York: Lyle Stuart.

ELLIS, A. (1976). The biological basis of human irrationality. *Journal of Individual Psychology* **32**, 145–168.

ELLIS, A. (1977). Intimacy in psychotherapy. *Rational Living* **12**(2), 13–19.

ELLIS, A. (1978). Toward a theory of personality. In Corsini, R.J. (Ed.) *Readings in Current Personality Theories*. Illinois: F.E. Peacock.

ELLIS, A. (1980). The philosophic implications and dangers of some popular behavior therapy techniques. Invited address to the World Congress on Behavior Therapy, July, Jerusalem.

ELLIS, A. and ABRAHMS, E. (1978). *Brief Psychotherapy in Medical and Health Practice*. New York: Springer.

ESCHENROEDER, G. (1979). Different therapeutic styles in rational-emotive therapy. *Rational Living* **14**(2), 3–7.

FRANK, J.D. (1970). Psychotherapists need theories. *International Journal of Psychiatry* **9**, 146–149.

GARFIELD, S.L. (1980). *Psychotherapy: An eclectic approach*. New York: Wiley.

GARFIELD, S.L. and KURTZ, R. (1977). A study of eclectic views. *Journal of Consulting and Clinical Psychology* **45**, 78–83.

LAZARUS, A.A. (1976). *Multimodal Behavior Therapy*. New York: Springer.

MORLEY, E.L. and WATKINS, J.T. (1974). Locus of control and effectivenss of two rational-emotive therapy styles. *Rational Living* **9**(2), 22–24.

NARDI, T.J. (1979). The use of psychodrama in R.E.T. *Rational Living* **14**(1), 35–38.

SHOSTROM, E.L. (1976). *Actualizing Therapy: Foundations for a scientific ethic*. San Diego: Edits.

WESSLER, R.A. and WESSLER, R.L. (1980). *The Principles and Practice of Rational–Emotive Therapy*. San Francisco: Jossey-Bass.

# Chapter 10
# Theoretically Consistent Eclecticism: Humanising a Computer 'Addict'

## My Unique Brand of Theoretically Consistent Eclecticism

Theoretically consistent eclectics are counsellors who have a particular theoretical perspective on human psychological disturbance but are prepared to use particular techniques developed by other counselling schools (Dryden, 1984a). In doing so they do not subscribe to the schools' theoretical postulates, but use techniques spawned by these schools for therapeutic purposes consistent with their own orientation. Although I consider myself a rational–emotive counsellor (REC) in that I am in basic agreement with the theoretical tenets of REC, I also consider myself 'eclectic' in that, in the *practice* of counselling, I select what appears to be best from diverse therapeutic sources, systems and styles to help my clients. The practice of theoretically consistent eclectics is likely to be quite individualistic in that these counsellors will draw from the aforementioned sources, systems, and styles what *they*, individually, consider to be best. What guides them in their choices is as yet unknown, and this area would be a fruitful one for research.

Before describing the case I have selected here, I wish to outline the major elements that constitute my own brand of theoretically consistent eclecticism.

### Rational–emotive counselling: my theoretical base

I am in basic agreement with the ideas of Albert Ellis (1984) concerning the foundations of psychological disturbance. REC posits that although emotions, cognitions, and behaviours are interdependent processes, much human disturbance seems to stem from absolutistic, evaluative cognitions

---

First published in 1987.

132

that profoundly affect how humans feel and act. These cognitions, which are often couched in the form of 'musts', 'absolute shoulds', 'oughts', 'have to's' etc., are termed 'irrational' by REC theory in that they frequently impede people from reaching their basic goals and purposes. One of the major tasks of REC practitioners is to help clients change their absolutistic evaluative cognitions to those which are non-absolutistic in nature. These latter cognitions are frequently couched in the form of 'wants', 'wishes', 'desires', 'preferences' etc., and basically help people achieve their basic goals and purposes and adapt constructively when these cannot be met.

REC practitioners have invented a whole range of cognitive, emotive and behavioural techniques that they routinely employ in counselling, but REC-oriented theoretically consistent eclectics, as mentioned above, go further and employ a number of techniques derived from other counselling schools to help clients effect a profound philosophical change, i.e. from devout absolute beliefs to non-devout relative beliefs. In my case, I often use methods and techniques derived from gestalt counselling, transactional analysis, personal construct counselling, behavioural counselling, person-centred counselling and Adlerian counselling, to name but a few. However, and this should be emphasised, I use REC as a guiding framework for the selection of appropriate techniques. In addition, REC helps me decide which techniques *not* to choose (Dryden, 1984b). In the case that follows I attempt to show how I use REC as part of my therapeutic decision-making in this regard.

## Therapeutic alliance theory

The second major element in my brand of theoretically consistent eclecticism concerns the application of what has come to be known as 'therapeutic alliance theory'. Although the term 'therapeutic alliance' has been in use in the literature for over 50 years, the concept has recently been reformulated by Ed Bordin (1979). Bordin has argued that there are three major components of the alliance between counsellor and client: *bonds*, *goals* and *tasks*.

Alliance theory proposes that effective counselling occurs when the bonds between counsellor and client are strong enough for the work of counselling to be executed. My overriding concern here is to develop a type of bond with a particular client that will enable me to help that person without unwittingly perpetuating his or her problems. There are two important elements here. First, most clients (if not all) come into counselling with implicit (or explicit) preferences for a particular type of relationship with their counsellor. Some, for example, seek a formal type of relationship, whereas others prefer one that is more personal and intimate. I seek to meet a client's preferences to the extent that they do not perpetuate his or her problem. As will be shown in the case to be described, the client sought a formal type of relationship with me, which, if offered, would have rendered me a less potent change agent. The second element, the relationship between the client's interpersonal style and his problems, is to be found in the writings of interpersonal counsellors (e.g. Anchin and Kiesler, 1982). These theorists argue that clients bring a preferred interpersonal style to counselling and 'pull' a complementary response style from their (unsuspecting) counsellors, which, in turn, reinforces both their own self-defeating style and their psychological problems. Thus, a client who presents herself as 'helpless' in counselling may well 'pull' an overly active–directive stance from her counsellor, which renders her more 'helpless'. Thus, I ask myself: 'What interpersonal style will enable me to keep this client in counselling [clients' disconfirmed expectations here may lead to premature termination] while at the same time helping him (or her) to escape his (or her) self-imposed vicious cycles?'

Secondly, the *goals* of the enterprise must be considered. Effective counselling is deemed to occur when counsellor and client agree on the latter's goals. Agreement on goals can occur at three levels:

1.  Client and counsellor can set *outcome goals*, which represent what the client wishes to achieve at the end of counselling.
2.  *Mediating goals* can be set. These are the goals that the client needs to achieve before outcome goals can be reached. For example, a client may have to become proficient in a number of social skills before realistically being able to achieve the outcome goals of finding a partner.
3.  Client and counsellor can set goals for a particular session (i.e. *session goals*).

Alliance theory predicts that effective counselling is facilitated by the participants' agreements on each of these goals (where appropriate) and when they both can see the progressive link between the three levels (i.e. session goals → mediating goals → outcome goals).

Thirdly, counselling *tasks* must be considered. Both counsellor and client have tasks to carry out in counselling. Alliance theory predicts that effective counselling is facilitated when each person: (1) understands what tasks he or she has to execute; (2) can see the relevance of the other person's tasks; (3) is able to execute his or her respective tasks; and (4) acknowledges that the execution of these promotes the attainment of the client's goals. In addition, the tasks must have sufficient therapeutic potency to facilitate goal achievement. Thus, as a theoretically consistent eclectic, I need to know that the techniques I select from other therapeutic schools are sufficiently powerful vehicles to promote therapeutic change. For example, exposure methods may well help clients overcome phobic reactions, but Gendlin's (1978) focusing techniques probably will not.

Finally, a channel of communication needs to be established between counsellor and client so that alliance issues can be discussed and problems in the alliance resolved (see Chapter 3).

## Challenging but not overwhelming

The third major feature of my eclectic approach is based on a principle that I have come to call 'challenging but not overwhelming' (Dryden, 1985). I believe that people learn best in an atmosphere of creative challenge, and I try to develop such an environment for my clients in counselling (Hoehn-Saric, 1978). Conversely, people will not learn as much in a situation that either challenges them insufficiently or over-whelms them. In this respect, Hoehn-Saric (1978) has shown that a productive level of emotional arousal facilitates therapeutic learning. For example, some clients are emotionally overstimulated, and hence the counselling task is to create a learning environment that decreases their emotional tension to a level where they can adequately reflect on their experiences. With these clients, I make use of a lot of cognitive techniques and adopt an interpersonal style that aims to decrease affect. This style may be either formal or informal in character. These strategies are particularly appropriate with clients who have a 'hysterical' style of functioning. However, other clients require a more emotionally charged learning atmosphere. Such clients often use 'intellectualisation' as a major defence and are used to denying feelings (see the case to be described). With such clients I attempt to inject a productive level of affect into the counselling session and employ emotive techniques, self-disclosure and a good deal of humour. These 'challenging' strategies are best introduced gradually so as not to overwhelm clients with an environment they are not accustomed to utilising. However, before deciding on which interpersonal style to emphasise with clients, I routinely gain information from them concerning how they learn best. Some clients learn best directly through experience whereas for others vicarious experiences seem to be more productive. I try to develop a learning profile for each of my clients and use this information to help me plan my counselling strategies and choose techniques designed to implement these strategies. Care needs to be taken, however, that the counsellor does not use a mode of learning that may perpetuate the client's problems.

The 'challenging but not overwhelming' principle extends to Ellis's (1979, 1980) writings on 'discomfort anxiety'. Ellis has argued that many clients perpetuate their problems and deprive themselves of learning experiences because they believe that they *must* be comfortable. Thus, a major counselling task here is to help such clients challenge this belief and carry out assignments, while tolerating their uncomfortable feelings.

Although this is a sound theoretical principle, I have found that it needs to be modified for pragmatic purposes. It may be desirable for a client who is anxious about eating in public to go to an expensive restaurant and challenge her anxiety-creating cognitions in a situation where her worst fears may be realised, but many clients will not do this. When I provide a rationale for homework assignments, I do so in a way that incorporates the 'challenging but not overwhelming' principle and contrasts it with gradual desensitisation and implosion methods:

> There are three ways you can overcome your fears. The first is like jumping in at the deep end; you expose yourself straightaway to the situation you are most afraid of. The advantage here is that if you can learn that nothing terrible will happen, then you will overcome your problems quite quickly. However, the disadvantage is that some people just can't bring themselves to do this and get quite discouraged as a result. The second way is to go very gradually. Here, on the one hand, you only do something that you feel comfortable doing, while, on the other, you don't really get an opportunity to face putting up with discomfort, which in my opinion is a major feature of your problem. Also, treatment will take much longer this way. The third way is what I call 'challenging but not overwhelming'. Here you choose an assignment which is sufficiently challenging for you to make progress but not one which you feel would be overwhelming for you at any given stage. Here you are likely to make progress more quickly than with the gradual approach but more slowly than with the deep-end approach.

I find that when clients are given an opportunity to choose their own rate of progress, the therapeutic alliance is strengthened. Most clients choose the 'challenging but not overwhelming' approach, and only very rarely do they opt for the gradual desensitisation approach. When they do so, I try to dissuade them and frequently succeed. In the final analysis, however, I have not found it productive to insist that clients choose a particular way of tackling problems that is against their preferences.

Having outlined the major elements of my eclectic approach, I shall now describe the case I have selected to demonstrate my approach in action.

# The Client

The client, whom I shall call Eric, was a 31-year-old, white, unmarried man. He was born in the south of England, an only child of Peter and Margaret. His father was a ranking officer in the British Army and his mother did not work outside the home. At the time of treatment, Eric lived alone in a flat in Birmingham and worked as a computer programmer in a middle-sized business institution that manufactures electronic equipment. He was educated at a leading British university and has a master's degree in computer studies.

Eric sought counselling because he had increasingly come to feel that his life lacked direction and he had recently become concerned about his

level of alcohol intake. This was the first time that he had sought help and there was no evidence of any psychiatric history. He enjoyed good physical health.

He initially reported his childhood to be uneventful; he saw his father infrequently because of the latter's Army commitments and described his relationship with his mother as 'cordial but rather distant'. He was sent to boarding school at the age of 10 where he remained until age 18, when he went to university. He said that he had many acquaintances at boarding school and university, but no real friends. He dated infrequently and reported no intimate relationships with women. He was sexually inexperienced and recently lost his virginity after having sex with a local prostitute. Describing this experience, he said, 'It was time, I thought, that I had sex with a woman; I felt a bit stupid being a 30-year-old virgin. I didn't enjoy it and wondered what all the fuss was about.' His main interest was in computers. He was fascinated by them and often worked late into the night trying to solve a problem posed by the latest program he was working on. Of late, however, he said, 'I can't seem to dredge up the enthusiasm any more.'

He was recommended to see me by his local GP, who gave him the name of a number of counsellors in the area. Explaining his choice of counsellor, Eric said: 'I chose to come and see you because I was attracted by the name rational–emotive counselling. I see myself as basically rational, but there seems to be a breakdown in my logic at the moment. I'm hoping you can isolate the bugs in the system.' Perhaps not surprisingly, Eric's language reflected his interest in computers. My immediate impression of this tall, well-groomed man was that he had almost become an extension of the computer he had recently lost interest in. His speech was very precise and his language lacked emotionally toned words. He was almost devoid of affect apart from allowing himself a little laugh when he drew attention to the fact that his surname was the same as a leading computer company.

His expectations for counselling were as follows. He anticipated that we would have an orderly discussion of his life's goals and why he had become 'stuck'. He further hoped we would find out why he had started drinking more heavily than was his custom. He was pleased that I was not going to ask him to lie on the couch: 'I like to see who I am talking to.' I was left with the initial impression that here was a man who kept a very tight rein over his feelings from which he had become increasingly divorced. He seemed to employ intellectualisation as a major defence in his life. Yet the cracks were beginning to appear. This marked the end of the initial interview, at which time I offered to accept him for counselling. We would review progress after five sessions, which would give him an opportunity to determine whether I was the kind of person who could help him. He accepted this contract.

# The Counselling

What I shall do is to give an account of my work with Eric over the 17 sessions I saw him. I will include at various points (1) my thoughts as a counsellor, which will help the reader understand my eclectic approach, and (2) verbatim transcripts of our interchanges to illustrate (a) Eric's mode of functioning, (b) two critical incidents, and (c) how I dealt with an incident concerning Eric's resistance to experiencing feelings.

## Initial phase (sessions 1–4)

Initially I asked Eric to help me understand more deeply his predicament and what he would like to achieve from counselling. He reiterated the theme first raised in the intake session, namely, that he wanted to regain his enthusiasm for his computer interest and was puzzled about what had been going wrong.

Initially I wanted to test my hypothesis that his difficulties lay in the feeling domain, so I decided to ask him to fill out a structural profile (Lazarus, 1981) to test this and to demonstrate to Eric how he saw himself as a person.

### Session 1 transcript (client functioning)

**Windy:** Okay, Eric, now throughout counselling I'll be sharing some hunches with you, and it would be good if you could help us both by giving me honest reactions to these hunches. I see you and myself as a team joining together to figure out what has gone wrong in your life and how you can find a more meaningful direction for you. How does that seem?

**Eric:** Fine.

**W:** Now, human beings have seven basic aspects. These aspects interact with one another to be sure, but I want to understand how you see yourself on these aspects. I want to use a rating scale from 0 to 10, 0 being an absence of this modality and 10 being a high score on it. Now these modalities are behaviour, affect, sensation, imagery, cognition, interpersonal relationships, and biological factors.* Now taking behaviour first...

I then spent some time developing the structural profile with Eric (Figure 10.1).

**W:** Okay, what's your reaction to this profile?

**E:** What do you mean?

**W:** Well, can you see anything that might be related to your current difficulties?

**E:** Mmm. Well ... I'm not sure.

**W:** Okay, let me share my reaction. I'm struck by the low scores on affect, sensation and interpersonal relationships. For example, I wonder if you would benefit from experiencing more feelings in your life. Let's start with that.

---

*See Lazarus (1981) for a full description of the structural profile and how to use it in counselling.

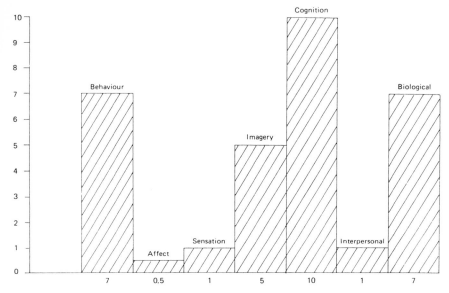

**Figure 10.1**    Eric's structural profile (session 1)

E:      Feelings? I'm not sure what you mean by that.

W:      Well emotions like joy, guilt, happiness, sadness, anxiety, depression, pleasure.

E:      Well, I used to get pleasure out of my computer, but the others? I ... er, I'm not sure. I'm puzzled by that. Aren't feelings biological processes that originate in the hypothalamus or is it the thalamus?

W:      [ignoring the temptation to discuss the psychophysiology of emotion]: You seem to be finding it difficult to relate to these emotions.

E:      Yeah.

W:      Well, is this an area we need to explore?

E:      [doubtfully]: I suppose so.

A similar dialogue occurred on the topic of sensations with Eric speculating on their biological origins rather than on his experience. Following is the interchange concerning Eric's interpersonal relationships.

W:      Now how about your relationship with people?

E:      Well, I've never sought people out.

W:      Have they sought you out?

E:      No.

W:      How do you feel about that?

E:      What do you mean?

W:      [noting the client's puzzled response to another feeling-oriented question]: Well you describe your life as being empty of people. What do you think your life would be like if there were more people in it?

E:      It would distract me from my computer work.

W:      So you wouldn't like more people in your life?

E:      I wouldn't know what to *do* with them.

The above excerpt shows Eric's dilemma. Feelings are alien experiences and people are either an unwelcome distraction or a puzzle. He doesn't know what to *do* with them. I remember experiencing something of a dilemma myself at this point. How can I help this man entertain experiences that are so alien to him?

I decided to share my dilemma in session 2 when we were talking about goals. This was an error since Eric could not relate to what I said to him. However, when I asked him, 'Could these areas be the bugs in your system?' he reacted with visible (although transitory) alarm. I remember thinking that I was going to have to use his language to build the bridge between his affectless world and one that held the most promise for him. An investigation into how Eric best learned revealed an overreliance on books, radio and television. These would clearly be of little relevance in our counselling work since these media could well reinforce Eric's detachment and intellectualisation. Other learning modes would have to be gradually introduced.

Although I like to set treatment goals early in counselling, I decided to postpone goal-setting for a while and work in a less structured way with Eric for two reasons. First, I did not consider that he would benefit from an early discussion about goals since he could not yet relate to issues about feelings, sensations and relationships. Secondly, I considered that he would initially benefit more from a more open-ended exploration. This would help him to widen his horizons and to loosen up a little.

In session 3 we talked about his thoughts concerning his structural profile and the 'bugs in his system'. He noticed that he tended to drink more at those times he found himself thinking about our sessions. I suggested that he refrain from drinking to experience whatever it was that he might be feeling at those times. I taught him Gendlin's (1978) focusing technique to help him in this regard. This technique is particularly helpful in that it directs clients' attention to their inner sensations and experiences and helps them to articulate what these experiences might be about. In session 4 I helped Eric to attach a feeling label to his experience. He was feeling sad. I helped him to realise that sadness can be a cue that there was something missing from his life, perhaps something other than computers. He nodded imperceptibly in agreement, but wondered what that was. I suggested it was our task to help him find out.

Up to now I would describe my approach to Eric as basically exploratory. I was beginning to 'challenge' him to look at his inner experience, but not in a way that would 'overwhelm' him and possibly scare him away. The two techniques I used in this initial phase were designed to help both of use move into what was for Eric the uncharted waters of his inner world. Neither of us could see at this stage that the next session would be so critical in the counselling endeavour.

## Middle phase (sessions 5–14)

While reviewing my notes a few days prior to my fifth session with Eric, I noticed that Eric would have his thirty-second birthday on the day of this session. I let my mind wander and experienced a sense of sadness. I pictured Eric on his birthday alone in his flat and guessed that nobody would send him a birthday card. I decided I would buy him a card, which I would give him at the beginning of the session. My decision was prompted by a sense of empathy, but I also reflected on the therapeutic wisdom of doing so. Would he despise me for my open display of caring concern? Would he be affected? What might he experience? Empathy won the day, although I was somewhat apprehensive when I sat down at the beginning of the session. I want to stress that I did not see this purely as a technique. If I did not experience the concern, I would not have given him the card. The following are excerpts from the session.

*Session 5 transcript (critical incident)*

**Windy:** Eric, I noticed today was your birthday and I felt that I would like to give you this [handing over the card].
**Eric:** [puzzled]: What is it?
**W:** Why don't you open it?
**E:** [opening the envelope]: Oh! Er ... um ... I don't know ... what to say.
**W:** You seem agitated.
**E:** [clearly embarrassed]: Yeah ... well ... that's ... a ... well ... um [bursts into tears].

Eric wept silently for about 5 minutes and was clearly distressed. I felt both touched and concerned lest this was too overwhelming an experience for him at this point.

**W:** When was the last time you received a birthday card?
**E:** [distracted]: What? ... er ... well, let me ... see ... er ... I can't remember.
**W:** When I decided to buy you the card, I felt kind of sad because I guessed that nobody would have sent you one.
**E:** Pathetic isn't it.
**W:** What is?
**E:** Weeping like a baby over a silly card. Oh! I didn't mean ...
**W:** I know what you mean. How do you feel about weeping with sadness?
**E:** I feel bloody stupid.

The rest of the session was spent helping Eric to see that he could accept himself for crying and that his sadness was perhaps an indication that some important desires were not being met. However, Eric remained somewhat distracted and I used these strategies to decrease the intensity of his experience (which I hypothesised would have otherwise been overwhelming for him) as well as a method of disputing his irrational belief: 'I am worthless if I cry.'

Towards the end of the session, I wondered aloud whether Eric would find it difficult to come back next session having expressed some strong feelings. He nodded, and I said that I understood that feeling.

Indeed, Eric did not show up for session 6. I was concerned about him, particularly as he did not call to cancel his appointment. I decided to write the following letter:

> Dear Eric,
> I was sorry that you were not able to attend our session on Wednesday. My hunch is that you feel embarrassed about our last session. If I am right I can understand you feeling that way. If you recall, I mentioned at our second session that counselling can be difficult at times and there might be occasions when you might not want to come.* However, I feel it is important for us to talk about these experiences in person, so I look forward to seeing you for our next session at the same time next week. Please confirm that this arrangement is convenient.
> Yours sincerely,
> W. Dryden, PhD

I received a reply from Eric, thanking me for my letter and confirming that he would attend our sixth session. The following is an excerpt from this session.

### Session 6 transcript (critical incident)

**Eric:**  You know, when I got home, I found myself with a whisky bottle in my hand before I even knew what was happening. I remembered what you said about not drinking to see what feelings came up. I was overwhelmed with stomach cramps and I began to cry again. Somewhere at the back of my mind I remembered you asking me if I was worthless for crying. I was able to see that I wasn't and for the first time I let go. I cried and cried. I remembered my father saying things when I was a child like: 'Call yourself a boy, stop those tears.' I also remembered my mother getting agitated because I was crying and my father was due home soon.

**Windy:**  Sounds like a lot of hidden feelings came up for you.

**E:**  Yeah. When last Wednesday came, I panicked. You were right, I couldn't face you then. I went to my computer. I realised that I'd been using it as a friend, someone . . . something rather . . . that I could relate to . . . I also remembered what you said about your challenging but not overwhelming principle. I'd had enough challenge for a while and needed to have a rest. Sorry I didn't let you know.

[And later in the session. . .]

**E:**  I can see more clearly that I do need to get to know about some of those modalities that were low; you know, affect and the others. That's what I'd like to focus on.

At the end of the sixth session I suggested that Eric think about what kinds of experiences he would like to seek out. He came back with the following list at session 7.

---

*I frequently tell my clients that there may be times when they may wish to miss sessions. I do this partly so that I can remind them of the fact if and when the 'going gets rough' for them.

1. Learn to dance.
2. Find myself a girlfriend (about time!).
3. Go walking in the woods.
4. Join 18+.*

Eric devised his own programme and followed it through according to the 'challenging but not overwhelming' principle with good success. On a number of occasions he chose not to go to an event, using his computer as a kind of anxiety-reduction technique.

Mindful of the importance of using emotively oriented techniques to help Eric, I employed a number of these methods to help him focus on avoidance behaviour.

For example, in session 9, Eric reported that he couldn't be bothered to go to 18+ on club night and spent the evening working on his computer. I decided to use a gestalt empty-chair technique to dramatise the situation to enable Eric to identify any possible anxieties.

### Session 9 transcript (using a dramatic method to uncover the meaning of Eric's avoidance behaviour)

**Windy:** Let's see if we can understand whether you were avoiding some important feeling. Now let me explain a drama technique to you. First, can you imagine how you were feeling that night?

**Eric:** Er ... yeah ... tired.

**W:** Okay. So one of the players in this play is 'Tired Eric'. Now another one is your computer. (Can you imagine Tired Eric talking to his computer?)

**E:** [laughs]: Just about.

**W:** Good. Now, see this empty chair? Imagine your computer on that chair. Got it?

**E:** Yeah.

**W:** Now strange as it might seem, I want you as Tired Eric to talk to your computer. And I'll play myself in this. Okay? Right. Okay, Tired Eric, it's time to go out to 18+.

**E:** [as Tired Eric]: I'm too tired.

**W:** [to computer]: Is Eric too tired or might he be feeling something else? Eric, change chairs and answer me as your computer.

**E:** [as computer]: Well, no, he's scared.

**W:** [to computer]: Scared of what?

**E:** [as computer]: Well, he's got his eye on a girl at the club but he's scared she might not want to know him.

**W:** [to computer]: So why don't you tell him to go and face his fears.

**E:** [as computer]: Er ... because ...

**E:** [as Tired Eric and changing chairs after being prompted by the counsellor]: I know, because he doesn't think I'm strong enough to cope with rejection.

**W:** [to Tired Eric]: Is that true?

**E:** [as Tired Eric]: No, but why risk it if it's a possibility?

---

*18+ is a national social club for people between the ages of 18 and 30. A number of the members, however, are older than 30. It has branches throughout the UK.

This dialogue helped Eric and myself see that two important beliefs were holding Eric back. One was 'I'll only do things if they are certain to work out' and the other was 'If I do things and they don't work out, I'm no good.' I then helped Eric to dispute these beliefs using traditional REC disputing methods. He considered a more healthy alternative to both beliefs to be 'Things won't work out if I don't try. So I'd better increase the chances of getting what I want by going for them. If they don't work out, tough. I'm no less a person.' Eric practised these new beliefs by acting on them. He carried out a number of homework assignments between sessions 9 and 11 which were designed to help him accept himself in the face of failure and to help him work toward goals, the achievement of which could not be guaranteed.

In session 12 it emerged from reviewing these assignments that Eric feared losing control if he experienced strong arousal. His belief here was 'If I get excited, I'll lose control and that would be awful'. In order to test out the prediction that he would lose control if he experienced a lot of arousal, Eric did several things between sessions 12 and 14. He did a number of shame-attacking exercises (Dryden, 1984b). For example, he went into a large department store and shouted out the time. In addition, in session 13, I got him to sprint up and down on the spot and then do a number of expressive meditation exercises designed to raise his arousal level. Finally he went to a dance-therapy workshop and did a lot of vigorous dance exercises. All these experiences helped him to see that he could get highly aroused without losing control.

By session 14, Eric considered that he had made a lot of progress. He was feeling more in touch with his emotions, the range of which had markedly increased. He gained pleasure from walking in the country and enjoyed experiencing a variety of country odours. He had taken up bird watching and had found a girlfriend who also enjoyed these activities. He had made several friends at the 18+ club and was experimenting with a wide range of activities. His enthusiasm for his computer work had returned, but he spent far less of his recreational time at his computer terminal.

### End phase (sessions 15–17)

Eric suggested at the beginning of the fifteenth session that he would like to come less frequently and work towards termination. I outlined a number of ways we could terminate our work together. He chose to come twice more at monthly intervals. We spent these final sessions reviewing our work together, and Eric reported that he had maintained the gains he had made in counselling. At the end of session 16, I suggested that Eric might bring to our last scheduled session a written account of what he had achieved in counselling. The following is a verbatim account of what he wrote under the heading, 'What I Gained from Counselling'.

### What I gained from counselling

I have gained a great deal from seeing you, far more than I thought I would. You have opened my eyes to a whole new world of experience that I was only dimly aware of, if at all. I would say first and foremost I feel a more complete human being. Although I still respect my intellect – or the cognitive domain as the American man who invented those sheets calls it – I have learned to experience and gain respect for the other modalities. I have learned that it isn't unmanly to cry and feel sad. I've tried to discuss this with my father, but perhaps predictably he doesn't understand what I'm talking about. I have learned that it's not so bad to try and achieve something and fail. Indeed, if a person doesn't try, he certainly won't achieve. Obvious now, but I didn't see that before.

I have also learned that control has little to do with feeling strongly aroused. To some degree, looking back, I was using my computer to shield me from life, although of course I didn't realise that then. I guess I was using my computer as a substitute friend and yet it was a bit of a one-sided friendship. I now feel much more a part of the social world. 18+ has helped tremendously in that respect. Before I wouldn't have thought I could have so much fun with others. I didn't even think of life as having fun. Strange isn't it! I still have to force myself to go out occasionally when I feel 'tired' but I can now distinguish between genuine tiredness and anxiety.

I've redone those modalities (Figure 10.2) and have enclosed them within. I find the differences interesting. One last thought, I remembered

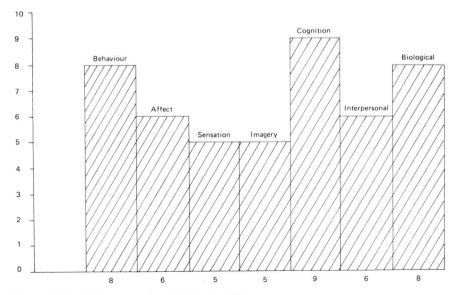

**Figure 10.2**   Eric's structural profile (session 17)

being struck by the name of your counselling before I came to see you – rational–emotive counselling. I was attracted to the word 'rational'. I must confess that I'm now more attracted to the word 'emotive'. I hope you find this instructive.

At the end of the seventeenth session, Eric and I agreed to have two follow-up sessions, the first one being 12 months after our last session. However, this has not yet taken place at the time of writing.

### Counsellor's summary

From the point of view of REC, Eric had developed an unsatisfactory lifestyle partly because he had little experience in the affect, sensation and interpersonal modalities but mainly because he held a number of irrational beliefs which led him to avoid experiences in each of these area. Namely he believed:

1. 'Experiencing emotions and sensations is extremely dangerous and must be avoided at all costs.'
2. 'I must be in control of myself. To lose control would be terrible.'
3. 'I must be certain of achieving something before I try it.'
4. 'I'm no good if I cry or if I fail to achieve important things.'

Adopting a theoretically consistent eclectic view based on my rational–emotive conceptualisations, I decided to emphasise strategies and techniques that were dramatic, affective and expressive in nature. In doing so I was sensitive to avoid overwhelming the client, but to challenge him gradually at first and later increasingly so as counselling progressed and as he began to make significant gains. Thus I decided to use:

1. *Structural profiles* as an assessment tool to help test my hunch about important deficits and to help Eric learn about these deficits.
2. Such techniques as *focusing* to help Eric to identify feelings and articulate what these feelings pointed to.
3. *Gestalt, two-chair dialogue* – to help him identify the meaning behind his avoidance manoeuvres.
4. *Dramatic mediation* and *dance therapy* – to help him learn that strong affective experiences were not dangerous and did not threaten his sense of control.

All these methods were chosen in line with strategies consistent with my REC-inspired formulation and in keeping with my hunches about the importance for Eric of learning to become accustomed to the experiential–affective domain of human functioning.

From the point of view of alliance theory, I was able to develop a well-bonded relationship with Eric. Initially he viewed me as a rather distant 'expert' who would help him iron out the 'bugs' in his system. The birthday card incident confronted him with the fact that I was also a human being who cared about his plight. This touched a deep cord in him and seemed to help him relate to me in a more affective manner. From session 6 our relationship was characterised by mutual respect and trust. I related to Eric in a moderately warm, informal manner without us both losing sight that we had various tasks to achieve.

With respect to the goal domain, I deliberately refrained from setting concrete goals at the outset of counselling. Initially, Eric wanted to pursue goals which, in my opinion, would have not been constructive for him. He wished to strengthen his intellectualised defences and rid himself of the 'bugs' in his system, which he hoped would help him shut out his increasing sense of isolation and dissatisfaction and hence to return to his computer. I did not attempt to deal explicitly with the self-defeating nature of these goals at the outset. I considered that to do this would have been unproductive and might have led to a futile 'intellectual' discussion, which I wanted to avoid. There was also evidence at this initial stage of counselling that Eric would not have understood the importance of goals that emphasised becoming increasingly aware of his feelings and the healing aspects of interpersonal relationships. Instead, I sidestepped the issue of goals by showing Eric the importance of looking at himself as a total individual (by using the structural profile) and how he was living his life against this backdrop. To some degree I think that Eric went along with me because he viewed me as an expert who knew what he was doing and because he was not too insistent about meeting his initial goals. Specific goal setting followed Eric's increasing understanding of the importance that the affective, sensation and interpersonal modalities might play in his life.

As Eric gained this understanding, it was fairly easy to show him that the execution of various tasks could help him achieve his newly discovered goals. The more Eric derived benefit from being able to experience feelings, sensations and the pleasure of relating to other people, the more he was able to see the sense of the evocative techniques that I suggested to him and how they could help him achieve his goals. Interestingly enough, we rarely had to talk *about* the relevance of counselling tasks; I believe he and I developed an implicit and shared understanding about these matters.

Following Bordin (1983), I believe that the repair of rifts in the therapeutic alliance can be most therapeutic. That Eric and I were able to sustain our relationship through the birthday card and the missed-session incidents was, I believe, important for a number of reasons. I consider that Eric learned from these two incidents that the expression of strong feelings (i.e. his feelings) could be tolerated by another person and by himself and that no catastrophe would result. I also think that Eric learned it was possible to talk about relationships with another person with whom he was involved and that rifts in these relationships can be repaired when both people show 'good faith'.

Applying the 'challenging but not overwhelming' principle to the case, I would like to make the following points. First, I attempted to provide a therapeutic environment that was increasingly charged with affect to encourage Eric to develop his potential to use the affective, sensory and interpersonal modalities. In this sense, I tried to challenge Eric's use of intellectualisation as a defence against such experiences without over-whelming him in this regard. The birthday card gift could have been an overwhelming experience for Eric, and to some extent I underestimated the effect that it would have on him. However, it was not a damaging experience for him, and indeed it contained important therapeutic ingredients for change (see the section on 'Client Impressions'). Secondly, I explained the 'challenging but not overwhelming' principle outlined earlier, with respect to the execution of therapeutic tasks, and Eric applied it to very good effect in his homework assignments. Indeed, as his own account in the next section shows, Eric has used this principle after counselling ended to maintain and extend his progress.

# Client Impressions

Two months after formal counselling had finished, I wrote the following letter to Eric:

Dear Eric,

I hope this letter finds you well. I have been asked by Dr J. Norcross of University of Rhode Island, USA, to contribute a case study to a book he is editing entitled *Casebook of Eclectic Psychotherapy*. With your permission I would like to write an account of our counselling and would like to request your permission for this. Your anonymity will of course be preserved.

If you agree, Dr Norcross also seeks to include the client's impressions of his/her counselling experiences. I would be grateful if you could write your impressions according to the following guidelines:

1. What were the most helpful and least helpful aspects of counselling?
2. What were your impressions of two critical incidents in counselling. Here I have selected (a) the session where I gave you a birthday card and (b) the session following the time you decided to miss our scheduled appointment (session 6).

Please feel free to be as candid as you can in your account. I look forward to receiving your reply upon which I will send you a copy of my account.

Yours sincerely,
W. Dryden, PhD

I received the following reply from Eric which I present as his verbatim account:

Dear Dr Dryden,

Thank you for your letter, You have my permission to write about our counselling work. I am pleased to offer my perspective of my counselling experience. I hope that it may be helpful to your colleagues and their clients. I would be interested to see your own account when you have finished it.

## Most helpful and least helpful aspects of my counselling

As I look back over the period of my counselling I can think of many helpful aspects but only one or two experiences that perhaps weren't very helpful. So my account is somewhat skewed to the positive. The most positive aspect of the counselling was the fact that you helped me discover the importance of feelings and personal relationships in my life. Until seeing you, I had not considered that these had any place in my life. Indeed, I had not really given these matters much thought. Why this should be so is difficult to say, but I suppose it had something to do with my father's attitudes towards feelings and the fact that my boarding school emphasised the value of hard work rather than the value of relationships between people.

Your suggestion that I refrain from drinking to help me discover what feelings I was hiding from and that focusing technique was particularly helpful in this respect. I also found some of the techniques you suggested that we try out together in our sessions helpful in aiding me to identify my feelings and some of the blocks I set up to stop me being uncomfortable. In particular, those meditation exercises were good and I still do some of them from time to time.

The other helpful aspects of my counselling were those exercises I did outside your office. I enjoyed immensely the dance workshop you suggested I attend. In fact I have joined a regular dance therapy group which I find valuable in helping me to overcome my tendency to what you called 'intellectualisation'. I didn't like that term when you first used it. I still don't like it but I know what you meant by it. I call it 'cutting out'.

The counselling helped me to make much better use of outside resources than I would have done without counselling. Counselling helped me to form some important friendships, in particular my relationship with my girlfriend June, which is still flourishing. Counselling was like a release in this respect.

Looking back I think your patience and understanding was very important (I'll mention your concern for me as a person later). Your easygoing manner was good for me although at the beginning, I'm not sure, but I think I would have preferred seeing an older man, one who was more formal in style and dress. I realise now that these things are unimportant though. I also found some of your explanations helpful. Your own principle of challenging but not overwhelming yourself was valuable, and I still use it as a guideline in my life.

Now some not so helpful aspects, although these are minor. First, at the beginning it might have been more helpful if you could have given me a clearer idea about what counselling was like. I was puzzled for about the first three sessions and was not sure what you expected me to do or say. Finally, it might have been more valuable if we could have spent more time talking about my childhood and my experiences at boarding school. I don't know whether that would have been helpful but I think that it might.

## Critical incidents

I can understand why you selected these two incidents. They stood out for me too. I was shocked when you gave me the birthday card — shocked and very embarrassed that I reacted in the way that I did. Your concern for me hit me between the eyes. I wasn't prepared for it and just did not understand at the time why I reacted so strongly. That experience really made me stop and think about my life. It made the meaning of the first profile I did come alive and helped me to see what I had been missing in life. I was, as you suspected, too embarrassed and ashamed to face you the week after. Your letter helped me to come back. You understood what I was feeling and again your concern was an important fact in helping me to return the following week. To be honest, if you had not written, I doubt whether I would have made the first move.

Coming back after the missed session was very important for me. You helped me feel that I wasn't a weak freak and also by not making too much of my missing the session you gave me important breathing space. Your matter-of-fact reaction gave me the impression that it was no big deal and also helped me think that you would not be shocked or startled by whatever I told you about myself. That attitude has remained with me and is also an attitude I can now apply to myself.

Well, I hope that you find these remarks of use. I'm very grateful to you for helping me in the way you did and am pleased to have had this opportunity to repay you in this small way.

Yours sincerely,

Eric

# References

ANCHIN, J.C. and KIESLER, D.J. (Eds.) (1982) *Handbook of Interpersonal Psychotherapy*. New York: Pergamon.

BORDIN, E.S. (1979). The generalizability of the psychoanalytic concept of the working alliance. *Psychotherapy: Theory, Research and Practice* 16, 252–260.

BORDIN, E.S. (1983). Myths, realities, and alternatives to clinical trials. Paper presented at the International Conference on Psychotherapy, Bogota, Columbia, February 1983.

DRYDEN, W. (1984a). Issues in the eclectic practice of individual therapy. In Dryden, W. (Ed.) *Individual Therapy in Britain*. London: Harper & Row.

DRYDEN, W. (1984b). *Rational–Emotive Therapy: Fundamentals and innovations*. Beckenham, Kent: Croom-Helm.

DRYDEN, W. (1985). Challenging but not overwhelming: A compromise in negotiating homework assignments. *British Journal of Cognitive Psychotherapy* 3(1), 77–80.

ELLIS, A. (1979). Discomfort anxiety: A new cognitive behavioral construct. Part 1. *Rational Living* 14(2), 3–8.

ELLIS, A. (1980). Discomfort anxiety: A new cognitive behavioral construct. Part 2. *Rational Living* 15(1), 25–30.

ELLIS, A. (1984). The essence of RET – 1984. *Journal of Rational–Emotive Therapy* 2(1), 19–25.

GENDLIN, E.T. (1978). *Focusing*. New York: Everest House.

HOEHN-SARIC, R. (1978). Emotional arousal, attitude change and psychotherapy. In Frank, J.D., Hoehn-Saric, R., Imber, S.D., Liberman, B.L. and Stone, A.R. (Eds.) *Effective Ingredients of Successful Psychotherapy*. New York: Brunner/Mazel.

LAZARUS, A.A. (1981). *The Practice of Multimodal Therapy*. New York: McGraw-Hill.

# Index